The
Historical
Present

The
Historical
Present

Uses and Abuses of the Past

Edwin M. Yoder

UNIVERSITY PRESS OF MISSISSIPPI / JACKSON

The paper in this book meets the guidelines for permanence
and durability of the Committee on Production Guidelines for
Book Longevity of the Council on Library Resources.

Library of Congress Cataloging-in-Publication Data

Yoder, Edwin.

    The historical present : uses and abuses of the past / Edwin M.
Yoder.

      p. cm.

    Includes bibliographical references and index.

    ISBN 0-87805-985-7 (cloth : alk. paper)

     1. United States—History—Philosophy. I. Title.

E175.9Y63 1997

973'.01—dc21   96-52057

                                                      CIP

British Library Cataloging-in-Publication data available

In grateful memory of three exemplary teachers of history:
JAMES ROY CALDWELL, JR.
PHILIP MAYNARD WILLIAMS
SIR EDGAR TREVOR WILLIAMS

Contents

Games Historians Play

Acknowledgments

When I first suggested this book to JoAnne Prichard, executive editor of the University Press of Mississippi, I said that it would be a labor of love. I meant that it would deal with a subject that has long fascinated me—that neglected crossroad where the past meets and illuminates the present. The resulting manuscript then went through several drafts, and I am grateful to Ms. Prichard, whose keen editorial eye saw the makings of a coherent book in the fragmentary raw materials I initially submitted. Her suggestions were invaluable.

As always, I owe a debt to my editors at The *Washington Post* Writers Group—Bill Dickinson, Alan Shearer and Anna Karavangelos—and to a number of editors of *Book World* over the years, especially Eve Auchincloss, Bridgitte Weeks and the late Reid Beddow. I have profited from conversations about many of the topics touched upon in this book with my colleagues at Washington and Lee, especially John Jennings, Holt Merchant and Hampden Smith III. As in the past, two valued friends, John Maurice Evans and Jonathan Yardley, read and commented on the manuscript. They spared me significant errors of judgment, taste and style.

I have dedicated this book to the memory of three mentors in the field of history. Jim Caldwell, known to many of his friends and colleagues in the history department at the University of North Carolina at Chapel Hill as "Speck," was my freshman instructor in both parts of the two-semester course in Western Civilization. It was from him, along with my father, that I had the good fortune to contract my earliest enthusiasm for the study of the past. I have written a somewhat longer portrait of this remarkable figure in my book *The Night of the Old South Ball*. Philip Williams, then a fellow of Jesus College, Oxford, tutored me in one of my two special subjects—nineteenth- and early-twentieth-century European political history. Although his own primary field was then postwar French politics, Philip was equally at home in continental history. Like his own teacher, D. W. Brogan, he commanded a dazzling, at times intimidating, fund of fine detail. From Philip, who was to become a cherished friend before his untimely death, I learned precision in the analysis of the past—not that mine ever equalled his. I shall not forget his comment on an essay I wrote for him on the origins of World War I in which I bore down on the Anglo-German naval rivalry. "That's okay," he said, "so far as it goes, but there are at least six other ways to argue the question." He then proceeded with clarity and economy to sketch the other six. Sir Edgar Williams, "Bill" to most of his close friends, was Warden of Rhodes House during my time at Oxford and after—friend and counselor to hundreds of Rhodes Scholars. A Merton College history don before the war, he became chief of intelligence to Montgomery and ended his army career as its youngest brigadier. His distinctions of intellect and wit—which are praised in Montgomery's memoirs—made him a celebrity and a power in Oxford. But he was also a compassionate, wise, witty, kind and sometimes astringent friend, and a shaping influence in my life. Were there more historians like these three, the study and teaching of history as a humane discipline would be in less trouble today.

Introduction

If American civilization had a starting point, it was that crystallizing moment in the summer of 1776 when three great men in Philadelphia drafted the Declaration of Independence. Jefferson, Adams and Franklin appealed to recent history to justify the act of rebellion against the king of England. That the history they invoked was highly colored and tendentious ("He has sent hither swarms of officials to harass our people and eat out their substance") is beside the point. America was, almost uniquely, a consciously historical creation—a "new order of the ages" caused by a train of events.

It therefore seems strange that a land so self-consciously historical in origins has so often resisted the historical mode of understanding itself or the world around it. I have puzzled over this curiosity for years, and once sought to explain it as follows:

> The United States, in certain striking ways, has been exempt from the harsher penalties of history. . . . Most civilizations learn in a hard school to view present events warily, as portending calamity; accordingly they scan the past for precedents and keys to understanding and avoidance. But calamity has not been the common American experience. America afforded so much space, so much elbow room, so many resources for unpunished plunder, that the consequences of error have been mild—so far. Plagues, bombing, famine, mass displacement of populations, holocaust, these tragic instructors of mankind, even in our century, are happily lacking. . . . I cannot claim to have originated this theory. Variations on the theme of American exemption and innocence have been played by most of our major historians and novelists, from Henry James to Vann Woodward.

This is a stab at the problem. But whatever explains it, it seems obvious that we Americans have a "thing" about history, a tendency to shy from it. The essays in this book thus go somewhat counter to a national allergy. As they will show, I myself am deeply persuaded that history—the past—is the mesh and matrix through which alone we understand the present, and that, conversely, present moods and preoccupations determine the ways in which we perceive (or misperceive) the past. The process is continuous and reciprocal. "Historical consciousness"—the phrase is that of the distinguished historian John Lukacs, and is the title of his great work of historiography—is in actuality the only reliable kind of consciousness we have.

I hasten to say that I am not a historian by trade or professional training, and these essays aren't historical as a learned monograph or lecture might be. They originate in the journalistic give-and-take of one who has been commenting on the news for a living for some four decades. They deal with the points at which past and present intersect. Historical specialists may find them breezy, so it is appropriate to emphasize again that they are a form of journalism—no more, but no less. When I was a student at Oxford, tutors could make no more withering comment on a student essay than that it was "journalistic." But I learned a long time ago that dismissive labels are of little intrinsic importance, apart from the merits of what they dismiss. The test is what the reader may find in these essays—especially the lay reader with an interest in the nexus between past and present and their mutual illumination.

The case of Christopher Columbus, the subject of one of these explorations, will do as well as any for a preliminary illustrative thought experiment in the bearing of the past on the "news" of the present. The great Walter Cronkite of CBS News made a practice of leaving the air each evening with the words "And that's the way it is. . . ," giving the date. Deciding how "it is" on any given day is the journalist's burden, a risky one. We journalists work, as the label suggests, in and for the day, *la jour*. What would a Cronkite of 1492, supposing him to be present with a camera crew and microphone at the landfall, have made of Columbus's appearance in a new world? "Columbus Lays an Egg" might be one journalistic possibility, were the reporter aware that the explorer had been look-ing for a route to the Far East and had "discovered" San Salvador. We can imagine other comic misperceptions, for it is only after a significant lapse of time that we can say whether our journalistic guesswork about the news was good or bad, wise or silly. Time alone brings perspective, and perspective alone is the catalyst by which the newsworthy becomes, or fails to become, the historical. Someone has said, catchily, that "journalism is the first rough draft of history." But strictly speaking, the claim is self-flattering non-sense. Many a rough draft, called news, pronounced "that's the way it is," is destined for oblivion, while whole worlds that escape the newshawk's radar will someday loom as earthshaking. The day's headline reports the transient bloviations of a politician destined for early obscurity, while somewhere in a remote laboratory some-one is conducting an unnoticed experiment fraught with a new des-tiny for millions.

Given this unstable but fascinating connection between past and present, it is an abiding mystery why so many Americans casually dismiss history and historical study as if they were disposable and uninteresting.

My earliest journalistic mentors, writers like William T. Polk of the *Greensboro Daily News*, Gerald Johnson of the *Baltimore Sun*, and Bernard de Voto of *Harper's Magazine*, were given to the use of historical reference and analogy. I caught the bug from them, and few things that I write are free of historical reference and allu-sion. Historical analogy can be risky, for in certain obvious ways, analogy does violence to the genius of history, whose fascination lies in novelty. The Yale critic Harold Bloom, in his book *The West-ern Canon*, says that the mark of what is destined to last in literature is "strangeness," and that is true as well of the salient features of the past. They are remarkable because they are different, striking, strange.

When I first became seriously interested in history, going on half a century ago, the great metahistorians, especially Arnold J. Toyn-bee, were in high fashion. Toynbee's emerging twelve-volume *A Study of History* sought to tabulate and categorize the dynamics of historical continuity and change from the ancient civilizations and cultures to the present. The ultimate plaudit of cultural popularity in the 1940s and 1950s was to be the subject of a cover story in *Time* magazine, and Toynbee was. His profile was written, interestingly, by Whittaker Chambers, later the accuser of Alger Hiss in a great spy case. Toynbee's reputation underwent a drastic deflation within a decade or so under the pricking of historians like Pieter Geyl and Hugh Trevor-Roper. They charged that Toynbee's sweeping comparisons and glib categorizations blurred useful differences, that he was a philosophical fatalist who scanted the importance of human will. And if Toynbee was a flop, obviously the even breezier uses of historical analogy by a journalist are a high-risk enterprise.

Of greater negative weight these days, however, is the sad fact that any dealer in journalistic history works in a denuded terrain. Many old reference points are fading. The curator of Mount Vernon recently remarked that he no longer assumes that schoolchildren visiting the first president's home on the Potomac will grasp references that "every schoolboy" once recognized: Mason Weems's mythic stories of how the young George Washington cut down a cherry tree in his father's orchard and was too honest to deny it, or how as a strong young man Washington could throw a Spanish milled dollar across the Rappahannock. (It is perhaps a mark of the same attrition of lore that so many tourists who know the story gaze across the half-mile-wide Potomac at Mount Vernon and decide that the story has to be fictitious—as indeed it would be if that were where Washington had spent his boyhood.)

"It is now entirely possible," the Harvard historian David Donald wrote several years ago in the *New York Times*, "to lead a happy and successful life without knowing when the Civil War ended or being certain whether Theodore Roosevelt preceded Franklin D. Roosevelt." Donald, preparing his American history lectures for a long-past fall term, concluded that it had devolved upon teachers of history to "disenthrall" their students of "the spell of history . . . help them see the irrelevance of the past" and help them grasp mankind's limited control of its destiny.

When Donald's seemingly defeatist essay about history teaching appeared, I too rudely rejoined that "if he believes what he says, four decades of history teaching have made retirement appropriate, as a punch-drunk boxer needs to hang up the gloves." This was unnecessarily uncivil, for Donald's despondency might well have reflected a passing mood brought on by the end of summer break. Or it might have been a sardonic Swiftian satire on undergraduate ignorance. After teaching hundreds of undergraduates at Washington and Lee University in recent years, I am more sympathetic. History is not often a meaningful dimension for today's undergraduates, any more than are certain other references once thought essential to literacy.

An illustrative anecdote. In a journalism opinion-writing seminar I teach twice each year, we were discussing one day Justice Robert Jackson's Supreme Court opinion in the 1952 steel seizure case. I had asked the students to read it because the topic was presidential war powers. What Jackson wrote in *Youngstown Sheet and Tube v. Sawyer* is among the classic articulations of their limits: "Just what our forefathers would have envisioned had they foreseen modern conditions must be divined from materials almost as enigmatic as the dreams Joseph was called upon to interpret for Pharaoh."

The reference to Joseph's powers of dream interpretation drew blank stares. It turned out that no one understood because no one had read the Book of Genesis—shocking to one of my vintage who grew up in the Bible Belt. In another journalism course, I asked the students to identify "Ulysses: 1922." One resourceful lad wrote: "A novel by James Joyce [so far so good] regarding the life and times of Ulysses S. Grant." He had conflated a lecture on book censorship with another about book publishing in the nineteenth century in which I mentioned that Mark Twain had acted as the publisher of Grant's memoirs. In the same course, I discuss, along with other technological changes that have affected media over the centuries, the application of steam power to newspaper presses in the first quarter of the nineteenth century. It was the earliest precondition of anything worth calling "mass media." The steam engine now strikes students, and even some colleagues, as a technology almost as esoteric as Chinese water clocks. These illustrations are examples, of no special value in themselves. But they underscore the need to teach history well and to bring more historical reference into our reflection on passing events.

The unimaginative teaching of history has too often left the impression that the study of history is a dreary task of memorizing obscure names, dates, treaties, chronological sequences, elections, dynastic successions—lists and categories of facts. Names and dates and events are the indispensable building blocks of history, but no more. History is essentially an *inquiry*, and usually an inquiry into the most absorbing of social phenomena—transformations.

Perhaps the most famous example is the transformation Edward Gibbon attempted to account for in *The Decline and Fall of the Roman Empire*, the first volume of which appeared in the year of the American Revolution. The barbarian triumph over Rome, the eternal city, has haunted historians from Saint Augustine to the present. "I have described the triumph of barbarism and religion," Gibbon wrote in summary of his thesis. That thesis has been hotly contested ever since, which is part of the fun.

Another fascinating transformation involves the origins of American nationality, to which I referred at the outset of this introduction—how a thinly settled fringe of seaboard colonies turned itself, gradually at first and then in a revolutionary spasm, into a self-consciously independent nation. And yet another: how did the medieval social and political system of the ninth to the thirteenth centuries that historians later came to call "feudalism" yield to the unified nation-state, in which the unit of political loyalty was no longer the local warrior-lord in his fortified place but a king embodying a nation? Was it gunpowder or ideology? A sudden alteration of consciousness? In Shakespeare's history play *Henry V*, the Englishness of Henry Plantagenet's army at Agincourt is shown as highly developed and articulated. Is this historical, or is it an Elizabethan playwright's rearward projection of the nationalism of his age, two centuries later?

There are many more of these transformations than one could well inquire into, still less master, in a lifetime of study. In the introductory course in "mass communication" cited above, I normally begin with a brief history of writing and its social effects. Pictographic writing, the earliest form, required so many symbols that literacy became the monopoly of a caste, often associated with priestly or magical authority. Its restrictiveness survived in classical

Chinese, with its fifty thousand characters and its select mandarin-ate. But the Greek alphabet made it possible for words to be built with twenty-six symbols representing, in combination, a few basic sounds and brought an exponential spread of literacy, at least when social norms and conditions permitted. It was at least as important as the invention of moveable type in the fifteenth-century age of Gutenberg.

These and countless other examples show that history cannot be "irrelevant," though some may suppose it so. The study of the past is the only way we have to understand ourselves, since personal experience, however cosmopolitan, is finite and must be supplemented by reading and reflection. Memory, social or personal, is the only frame of reference that enables us to decode the present, whether the process is as mundane as checking a date on the calendar or reading about a puzzling war in the Balkans or in the Caucasus. If we read in the morning paper about a terrible civil war in Bosnia-Herzegovina, our grasp will vary in intensity and depth with the reach of historical memory. If the anguish of the city of Sarajevo calls up no more than the memory of a recent winter Olympics (itself poignant enough), and not the assassination of a royal archduke in the summer of 1914, our grasp is to that degree weakened.

Ultimately, the case for the uses of history, in journalism and elsewhere, lies in direct relevance to our lives. If history isn't about instructing us for the human journey, what is it about? Such a question would be dismissed as naive in some sophisticated circles today. The study of history had to reach a high degree of professional specialization (as it steadily has done in the last century) before historians were assailed by crippling doubts of its practical relevance. Reading my favorites among the founders of narrative history—Gibbon, Macaulay, Froude, Henry Adams, Francis Parkman—I see no sign that they regarded their inquiries as other than useful and instructive. They wrote history with both confidence and style and enjoyed wide readerships. That was especially true of Macaulay's *History of England,* which the writer aspired to make as popular as novels; he was successful in doing so. "On the day in November 1848 when the first volume of Macaulay's *History* appeared," writes Sir John Plumb, "Ludgate Hill was jammed with carriages struggling to get to Messrs. Longman in Paternoster Row. Three thousand copies were sold in ten days and the pace began to increase rather than slacken." As Keats wrote of his Grecian urn, there was congruity between truth and beauty in the great narrative accounts of the past. When Henry Adams wrote his elegant *History of the United States During the Administrations of Thomas Jefferson and James Madison,* or James Anthony Froude his richly circumstantial *History of England,* they assumed that statecraft and religious practice reflected an urge for human self-expression that historians could usefully and artfully illuminate.

The building blocks of the pieces in this book are columns written for The *Washington Post* Writers Group, which appeared in the *Post* and a variety of other newspapers in the United States and abroad over the past fifteen years, along with book reviews and addresses. For the sake of narrative flow and to avoid repetition I have consolidated separate treatments of the same subjects, updated the references and adopted a present perspective.

The love of the past and fascination with historical comparisons that inspired these exercises are legacies of the eighteenth-century Enlightenment that also gave us the idea of progress. They draw as well on the Romantic impulse that found mystery and pleasure in the contemplation of old ruins. We try to measure the significance of our brief scene by seeking some human scale in history, the faces of people who were like us, yet not entirely so, and scenes and situations that are recognizable but also strange. In that interplay between past and present lies the glamour of history and the usefulness of what follows. That usefulness is, of course, for the reader to determine.

PRESIDENTS AND
OTHER AMERICANS

The Crimes of
Christopher Columbus

 ∾

MANY PROFESSIONAL HISTORIANS no longer believe in what Lynn
Hunt of the University of Pennsylvania has called "the master narrative" of the past—that is, history as an intelligible and thematic
story, unfolding by the usual rules of progress or decline. And that
especially is so when the history in question is suspected of contam-
ination by the Western imperialist perspective. The imperialists of
Christopher Columbus's time did not realize that they were being
imperialistic, any more than their medieval precursors realized that
they were practicing something called "feudalism." Both terms
were coined by historians or economists long after the fact.

In any case, historical relativism now sits enthroned, and the
nineteenth-century aspiration of Leopold von Ranke and other pio-
neers of archival history to capture the past "as it really was" seems
hopelessly naive, even presumptuous. What we have is a wilderness
of competing perspectives, none of which is sufficiently masterly to
drive any "master narrative." That being so, it might have been
foreseen by those who entertained high hopes for the 1992 quin-

centenary of Columbus's first voyage to the New World as an educational exercise that the anniversary would prove instead to be a colossal flop, whose most striking keynote was a carping moralism. Whereas before he was celebrated as the "discoverer" of America, Columbus was now demonized as an exemplar of European white male presumption, the prototype of all later oppressors of "people of color." Indeed, one might easily have concluded that Columbus's voyages constituted a great historical misfortune, even though they were the precondition of the prosperity, and even the existence, of many well-fed academics who found them so.

The retrospective roasting of Columbus reached some sort of peak, whether of political correctness or of absurdity it would be hard to say, when a Columbus descendant was appointed grand marshal of the 1992 New Year's Day Rose Bowl Parade in Pasadena, California. The announcement quickly put the descendants of Columbus's supposed victims on the warpath. "American Indians," the *New York Times* reported, "said his selection was an insult because Columbus's arrival in the Americas had resulted in genocide" (another anachronistic term, but like the others emblematic of the unself-conscious use of retroactive moral categories). The Rose Bowl sponsors, seeking to ease the outrage, quickly ran in Ben Nighthorse Campbell, a member of Congress and a Cheyenne chieftain, as co-grand marshal.

As this and countless other oddities suggest, the fate of Columbus in the five hundredth year of his Western Hemisphere landfall (let's be as neutral as possible) made a fascinating study in the dilemmas and uncertainties of the history trade today.

It was not always so, even relatively recently. Many of us grew up with the heroic version of the great explorer's place in history, derived in substantial part from Washington Irving's fanciful 1828 biography. We were taught to view Columbus as a dreamy young Genoan who spent hours as a youth gazing out to sea and asking himself why departing ships had a strange way of sinking from sight at the horizon. One day, according to this fable, he suddenly saw—eureka!—that the earth must be round, and, having interested the king and queen of Spain in that astonishing fact, he ventured forth in his three ships to challenge the delusions of a superstitious age.

It is a charming story, a parable of pertinacity. It is also, to be sure, historical nonsense. The sphericity of the earth was never seriously challenged in Columbus's time or any other since the rise of the first sophisticated Mediterranean civilizations. Indeed, it was because Columbus significantly underestimated the circumference of the earth that he thought he could reach Japan or some other Far Eastern landfall by sailing west. His geometry, using the term in its literal sense, was far inferior to that of the Egyptian and Greek astronomers of antiquity.

An alternative and more sophisticated Columbus fable greeted us when we moved beyond children's storybooks. It began with the lack of refrigeration and with the advent of sailing ships capable of pointing high enough into the wind to sail across the Atlantic. These two factors were catalyzed by the Turkish conquests of the Mediterranean basin and the resulting obstruction of ancient overland trade routes. By the late fifteenth century, the Turks had choked off the importation of spices that made food palatable. Just in the nick of time, the Spanish and Portuguese caravels appeared, with lateen rigging. With their superior ability to sail close to the wind, they became the vessels of choice for all the great voyages of discovery (that inescapable but now tainted word again).

When I made the point about the caravels in a Sunday opinion piece in the *Washington Post*, more than one reader challenged the assertion that lateen rigging enabled ships to sail closer to the wind than square rigging. The challenge was ironic, since I was relating what amounted to a high-tech historical fable to which the precise accuracy or inaccuracy of the point about the caravels was immaterial. But the Dutch sailor and author Jan de Hartog writes in his little book *The Sailing Ship* that "the earliest Portuguese and Spanish explorers could never have set out on their transoceanic voyages without the tools and knowledge . . . handed down by the Arabs [who] contributed the lateen sail, the first fore-and-aft sail in the history of navigation." Hartog is seconded by the distinguished medieval historian Norman Cantor: "The development of the lateen sail made it possible for ships in the Atlantic and Baltic coastal trade to tack against the wind, which the old square sails did not permit." Cantor surely overstates the point, by the way, since all tacking in ships of sail is "against the wind" at some acute angle to its eye.

Both these traditional treatments of Columbus—one from children's storybooks, the other from chronicles of technological advance and determinism—might be challenged. But both shared the feel of what, borrowing from C. S. Lewis, we might call "mere history," history as an attempt to explore and explain great transformations of the past. Both are free of the radical doubts that now assail historical inquiry. If, according to one nineteenth-century practitioner, history is past politics, it has become present politics today.

I can't help counting this as a distinct loss to human understanding, whatever political solace it may offer to those who believe that their race, ethnic group, or ancestors were scanted in the master narratives of yesteryear. In the old days you could argue—often vigorously—about what history meant, what lessons it taught, who its heroes and villains were and what overarching themes it presented. What was seldom radically doubted, as it certainly is today, was that history existed and could be shaped by inquiry and discussion into a more or less truthful consensus tale. But many historians, having despaired of master narratives, now seek refuge in what sometimes look like escapist alternatives. We saw a good bit of such alternatives during the Columbian quincentenary.

One of them takes what might be called the *French Lieutenant's Woman* view of history, recalling the John Fowles novel that comes to two different conclusions and asks the reader to decide which ending he or she prefers. In *Smithsonian Magazine*, Simon Winchester noted that a Philippine monument commemorating the death of Magellan in April 1521 satisfies, by clever equivocation, two radically opposing views of the voyager who first sailed around the world. On one side, the monument marks Magellan's death as a "European tragedy"; on the other, "it is seen as an Oriental triumph—a heroic blow struck for Philippine nationalism." So the issue becomes, not which it really was, or in precisely what measure it was both European tragedy and Oriental triumph at once, but which view suits your political, national or ethnic preconceptions.

An even more dubious alternative to the old master narrative is to be found in the substitution of fabrication and fantasy for history—call it, if you like, the Napoleonic view, inasmuch as the emperor is reported to have called history "a fable agreed upon." In the twentieth century, Napoleon's view has certainly been useful to conquerors and plunderers who took a propagandistic view of historical truth and found it convenient to label their conquests "co-prosperity spheres" or "*lebensraum.*"

During the 1992 Columbian year, readers of the *Washington Post* were treated to a sample of the "fable agreed upon" view of Columbus in a survey of new works of fiction. Of course, the rules of fiction differ from the rules of history. But it is significant that Columbus, according to the reviewer, tended to be portrayed as "a garrulous buffoon," "equal parts dreamer and schemer," a figure who "once he reaches the earthly paradise . . . slings a hammock . . . and occupies his time issuing ditsy edicts." In a novel called *The Dogs of Paradise*, Columbus is "accompanied on his first voyage by none other than Marcel Proust."

These are entertaining literary conceits. But the reviewer, Prof. Gustave Firmat of Duke University, strangely asserted that the various novelists whose jokes and jibes he cited were "only elaborating assertions made by the Admiral himself . . . [for] these novels are wedded to the chronicles of discovery and conquest, of which Columbus's journals and letters are the earliest example." According to Firmat, it was Columbus himself who established "a narrative protocol . . . for the liberal conflation of fact and fantasy," since it was the explorer "who came up with the notion that paradise was located on the top of a monumental nipple."

What, exactly, was Professor Firmat saying? What are the implications of his notion that Columbus was, in effect, the real precursor of magical fiction about himself? The issue is not whether Columbus was "not only the discoverer of America, but also its first and one of its strongest fabulists." The question, surely, is whether he intended to be any sort of "fabulist," and it may confidently be answered in the negative. Perhaps Columbus did imagine that the

Garden of Eden was in Central America, and referred in one of his letters to a New World island where people are born with tails. But is it historical or useful to treat these solemn fantasies as a "narrative protocol"? With the present burgeoning of radical agnosticism and relativism in the writing of history, especially among "new historicist" literary critics, the borders between history proper and magical realism have become disconcertingly porous. In the suggestion that the fantasists are merely aping Columbus himself, we hear the siren song of the age: the pervasive attack not only upon objectivity in history, but upon the feasibility of writing any reliable account of the past at all.

The traditional response of historians has been to assume that where we find the fabulous and credulous in the past we shall learn more if we treat them as clues to a world, since lost, whose mental settings and reference points were quite different from our own. We do not usually treat them as models—or "protocols" to use Professor Firmat's strange term—to be imitated to the further obscuration of the past.

Again, Columbus makes a good case study. By all accounts, including his own, he seems to have been a man of ponderous earnestness. He believed what he wrote, however silly his report on men with tails sounds to us. Mere history is necessarily always an attempt to enter sympathetically into the "other country" of the past, even when those who inhabited that country entertained views that strike us as strange or appalling, and the task is the greater when we deal with very remote people, five centuries past. The more diligently you try to see the past through the eyes of its natives, the harder it becomes to patronize it or them. The issue of Columbus's responsibility for the mistreatment of native peoples is a case in point. Certainly native peoples were exploited, and, moreover, slaughtered by contagions to which they weren't immune. Samuel Eliot Morison, the great Columbus biographer of the last generation, did not shy from the word "genocide" to describe this tragic outcome. Had Columbus or his royal sponsors willed this fate for native peoples, as the genocidal maniacs of our time did, the crime would be shocking. But it was not willed; quite the contrary, in fact. The Indians were viewed as prospects for religious conversion and, by the explicit command of Queen Isabella, were to be "treated very well and lovingly." No fewer than six priests accompanied Columbus on his second voyage. Their presence was doubtless more significant than the imagined novelistic presence of Marcel Proust.

To many a modern secular eye, missionary purposes signal arrogant presumption. But a historical view of Columbus requires due notice that in his day European Christendom was under siege from Turkish invasions. Its anxiety must in many ways have resembled the anxiety the West felt during the worst days of the Cold War. Now that we too have achieved what Columbus's day called a "reconquest," we have still greater reason to feel sympathy for its sense of seige. The metaphysical confidence that permitted Columbus to view Indians (and Jews, who were being expelled from Spain in 1492, when they resisted Christian conversion) as candidates for salvation may be repugnant, or at any rate as strange as his plan to turn the profits of his enterprise to a new crusade to retake the Holy Sepulchre from Muslim hands. These motives would not be deemed appealing by twentieth-century standards. But we too have certainties that will appear strange five centuries from now.

If you suffer from the fashionable compulsion to cut heroes down to size, Columbus makes an inviting target. But what is historically interesting about Columbus's voyages after five hundred years is not the way in which he anticipated the modern world. Modernity may have been in some sense an important consequence of his explorations, but it was wholly incidental to his purpose. Columbus was of a distinctly premodern cast of mind. Had he believed the estimates of the learned doctors of his era, he would never have dreamed of trying to reach the East by sailing west. Had he shared the enlightened ecumenicism of the National Council of Churches, he would never have dreamed of proselytizing noble savages. Like the conquistadors who followed him, Columbus was looking for riches. But for this unworldly man, the riches were but means to larger ends. He planned to dedicate his wealth to Christian missions, to the advancement of an invisible empire of the spirit, an empire which that age of metaphysical certainties deemed more real than gold or gems.

Closely examined, Columbus's vision bears little or no resemblance whatever to the world of magical realist fiction; the two are literally worlds apart. Marcel Proust was not a passenger on the *Santa Maria*. The flight from the master narrative impoverished the Columbus quincentenary, but that impoverishment is merely another sign of our refusal to face the difficult task of weighing and assessing our competing judgments about the past. Neither choosing your own slant nor converting history into amusing fable with take-your-choice endings can explain the complex urges that led explorers to cross uncharted seas five centuries ago. For that we need something more modest; we must have mere history.

Thomas Jefferson as
Secular Saint

WHEN HE PROJECTED his luminous six-volume biography of
Thomas Jefferson, Dumas Malone was teaching at the University
of Virginia, the site of Jefferson's great house at Monticello. There,
the docents still speak in their Virginian way of "Mr. Jefferson" and
of his calling "cyards" and his "gyardens." "In that community,"
Malone later observed, "they still talked of Mr. Jefferson as if he
were in the next room."

By comparison with the sage of Monticello, most other great
figures of the American past seem remote. His figure is familiar,
especially in his Virginia haunts. Descriptions of the physical Jefferson, who was tall (for his era) at almost six foot three inches, lanky,
sandy-haired, and freckled, suggest a mildness and softness of de-
portment and speech. He aimed for the homely touch. I judge this
informality to have been a persona deliberately assumed. He was
apparently as amiable as the frayed carpet slippers he wore even at
White House soirees and, like them, gave the impression of being
a bit down at the heels. Unlike the other affluent gentlemen of his

age and position, he wore hose of cotton yarn, not silk, and their loose fit was often remarked upon. Henry Adams, evoking Jefferson at the time of his inauguration as third president on March 4, 1801, quotes two notable descriptions. The first is by Senator Maclay of Pennsylvania, who remembered Jefferson as "a slender man [with] rather the air of stiffness in his manner. His clothes seem too small. . . . He sits in a lounging manner on one hip commonly, with one of his shoulders elevated. . . . His face has a sunny aspect. His whole figure has a loose, shackling air. He had a rambling, vacant look. . . . He spoke almost without ceasing but even his discourses partook of his personal demeanor . . . loose and rambling; and yet he scattered information . . . and some even brilliant sentiments sparkled from him."

The second is from Augustus Foster, secretary at the British legation, who portrayed Jefferson after four years as president, in 1804: "He wore a blue coat, a thick gray-colored hairy waistcoat lapped over it, green velveteen breeches with pearl buttons, yarn stockings, and slippers down at the heels—his appearance being very much like that of a tall, large-boned farmer."

No doubt the description—which makes him sound a bit like a Harlequin—would have pleased Jefferson, since a tall, large-boned farmer was just what he was, or what he wished to be thought. He was, of course, far more than a Virginia farmer; in any case he took delight in teasing British diplomatic emissaries. Augustus Foster may have been the butt of just such a tease. The famous slouch, the "shackling" and "shambling" posture, the habit of lounging on one hip, the borderline wardrobe, reflected, I fancy, Jefferson's notion of aristocratic nonchalance; while it may not have been a pose, it had about it more than a trace of calculated theatricality. In that way it echoed his prose style, which combined a classical eighteenth-century stateliness with harrowing references to revolution, bloodshed, "monkish supersitition" and the strangulation of priests.

Jefferson's political ideal was a nation of God-fearing farmers, led from their palatial rural seats by cultivated Deist gentry like himself and his friend and constant ally, James Madison. He hated, or affected to hate, cities (except perhaps for Paris), crowds, industrialism, capitalism, paper money, lending and public debt. (The latter was understandable, since he was chronically short of cash and must have depended more than he liked on creditors.) He affected to love the simple Arcadian life, although he himself was not simple and kept an elegant table, stocked with the best French vintages, in an elegant house. He was reportedly the first American host to serve his guests macaroni and ice cream, though not together.

Thus the private Jefferson. For a brief overview of the public man we may adopt his own standard. He directed that the obelisk marking his grave at Monticello—the earlier one was gradually worn away and was replaced by a larger one than he had originally wanted—associate him with three accomplishments: the Declaration of Independence, the Virginia Statute for Religious Freedom, and the University of Virginia, "the bantling of my old age," as he called it. Not a word of the many public offices he held—governor of Virginia, state assemblyman, minister to France, secretary of state, vice president and president. Perhaps his view was that immortality is reserved for unusual ideas and acts, not for placeholding, however distinguished.

Taking him at his word, the three monuments are an index to his historic significance. The Declaration of Independence is the most consequential of all the great American state papers, preeminent in a small class that would also include the Constitution, *The Federalist*, Jefferson's own First Inaugural Address, Lincoln's two inaugural addresses and the Gettysburg Address. When Jefferson heralded the arrival of government "deriving its just powers from the consent of the governed," in July 1776, it was far more than "the common sense of the subject," as he later called it. It was a great novelty, in scope if not in principle, alarming heresy in fact. Government based on unalienable natural rights and the consent of the governed is the creed professed by most of the civilized world today. That was far from the case then, when Aristotelian suspicion of democracy still held the field. The tradition passed from Jefferson to Lincoln, born in backwoods Kentucky fifteen years before Jefferson died. For Lincoln, the Declaration was the pole star: "I have never had a feeling politically that did not spring from the sentiments embodied in the Declaration," Lincoln declared in 1861.

And of course he echoed the Declaration to resonant effect, with important variations and riffs, at Gettysburg in November 1863. From there, the influence of the Declaration has widened. It inspired the Bandung Conference of 1955 and hence underlay the mid-twentieth-century anticolonial revolt. It is the legacy that inspired the journalist George Will to name Jefferson "man of the millennium" as our own nears its end. After canvassing the various finalists he had nominated—Machiavelli, Luther, Washington, Jefferson and Lincoln—and after stipulating that Einstein and Churchill were the men of the century—Will explained Jefferson's millennial preeminence in these words: "History is the history of the mind, of ideas. Jefferson was, preeminently, the mind of the Revolution that succeeded. It resulted in the birth of the first modern nation, the nation that in the 20th century saved the world from tyranny. . . . Jeffersonianism is what free men believe. Jefferson is what a free person looks like—confident, serene, rational, disciplined, temperate, tolerant, curious."

A case can be made that the Virginia Statute for Religious Freedom was, in terms of the American experience, a greater achievement than the Declaration. In a world frayed by sectarian strife, from Kashmir to Teheran, from Sarajevo to Belfast, who would now question the wisdom of separating church and state, or the dangers of theocracy? The Establishment Clause of the First Amendment mirrors Jefferson's ideas, and the case law deriving from it is now premised on Jefferson's letter to the Danbury Baptists, calling for "an eternal wall of separation" between church and state. The implications of this separation continue to be debated and are strangely problematical for many Americans, who do not seem to grasp the point, central to the Jeffersonian argument, that separation guards religion against dilution even as it safeguards private conscience from official oppression or indoctrination. Jefferson, as usual, could at times sound almost casual about the principle involved. What did it matter to him, he asked, if his neighbor worshipped one god or twenty? "It neither picks my pocket nor breaks my leg." It is a relaxed rationale for liberty of conscience, but who now doubts the good sense of it?

Finally, there was the University of Virginia, which was to embody Jefferson's personal dedication to the advancement of learning and, incidentally, of secularism and republicanism. Here began Jefferson's ultimate enshrinement as a cultural icon, which his biographer Merrill Peterson designates as paramount among the many Jefferson "images" that had emerged by the time of his bicentennial in 1943.

Admittedly, most of Jefferson's strictly political legacies are long gone and were fading in his lifetime. Decentralized government, based on a farming economy, was destroyed, as he feared it would be, by war, debt, depression and the rise of industrialism: the triumph of the economic ideas of his rival Alexander Hamilton. Even as president, Jefferson could not maintain his pristine doctrine of limited government. It underwent the subversive strain of practicality when he was offered, and bought, Louisiana. Likewise, the embargo on exports in his second term—designed to try to keep the fragile new America unentangled in the Napoleonic wars—required mighty assertions of executive authority for which the Constitution made no clear provision. It also stretched the Bill of Rights to the limit of its considerable elasticity. But the embargo was a failure and it lasted only a little over a year. It signaled the eccentricity and fallibility of the pure "Virginia" creed in national politics, although a certain nostalgia for it remains to this day.

It was long ago established, Jefferson's failures notwithstanding, that he of all great figures must be a paragon, his virtues magnified, his flaws discounted or lovingly cherished as the minute *craquelure* of a master painting. But secular sainthood has incited detractors, old and new, to dwell on the warts and flaws. One of the earliest was his cousin John Randolph of Roanoke, who took to calling him "St. Thomas of Cantingbury." Recent scholars like the legal historian Leonard Levy, in a polemical exploration of Jefferson's "darker side"—his inconsistencies as a civil libertarian—have noted that his political style fell short of his ideals. In fact, of course, Jefferson was no more a paragon or saint than any other statesman. He quit the Virginia governorship at the height of the Redcoat raid on Virginia, in what it is fair to call an "abdication." He made indiscreet remarks in private about George Washington, while serving in Washington's cabinet. He violated his own principles not only in the Louisiana Purchase and Embargo, but in the treason prosecution of his hated rival, Aaron Burr. These are only a sampling of the imperfections, to which it is de rigueur now to add that the author of the denunciation of slavery in the original draft of the Declaration and in *The Notes on Virginia* owned some two hundred slaves and, unlike Washington, made no attempt to free them at his death. There was also a time, as Merrill Peterson reminds us in *The Jefferson Image in the American Mind,* when unionists deplored Jefferson as the father of secessionism, a doctrine they traced to his Kentucky Resolution against the Alien and Sedition Acts of 1798. More recently still, his psychobiographer Fawn Brodie resurrected the old tale of his unlikely, and unproved, affair with the slave ingenue Sally Hemings.

But why, after all, should anyone as deeply immersed as Jefferson was in the turbulence of his era have to be deemed a paragon in the first place? Why do Americans need to shape a saint out of human clay? One clue surely lies in the exalted rhetoric that was his trademark. "I have sworn upon the altar of God eternal hostility to every form of tyranny over the mind of man" and "We hold these truths to be self evident: that all men are created equal . . ." In these words we hear the celestial melody of Enlightenment humanism. And even when Jefferson lets fly a bloodcurdling sentiment ("the tree of liberty must be watered from time to time by the blood of patriots and tyrants . . . its natural manure") the words have a pastoral resonance. When you compare the idealism of the words with the shabby compromises that statecraft demands, what happens? The result is the characteristic American insistence on isolating the two from one another—the supposed dirty work of politics from the ideals. It is a historical and political phenomenon bearing close resemblance to what psychologists describe as neurotic "splitting" and dissociation. We don't want our national heroes contaminated by political wheeling and dealing, and the result is a Jeffersonian image that is always a bit unearthly. After all, we could pick and choose. Devotees of safe, sedate rural conservatism found much to praise in the pastoral Jefferson whose "country" was Virginia, and who decried cities and debt—even as expansive nationalists celebrated the Jefferson who bought Louisiana and spoke of transforming it into a continent-wide "empire of liberty." Saints, I suppose, are in the world to give us trouble, and Jefferson was no exception. His earliest political detractors, the high Federalists, were not altogether wrong in their wariness of Jefferson's taste for glowing abstractions, or in finding in it just a trace of hypocrisy.

When I worked as an editor for Joe L. Allbritton, then the owner and publisher of the *Washington Star*, he never tired of teasing me about the print of the "lost" Gilbert Stuart portrait of Jefferson that I had hung on my office wall or about Jefferson the man. Jefferson, he insisted, had been a giddy, impractical fellow. Why, the clock in the foyer at Monticello was so ill designed that the weights had to be recessed through holes in the floor. Surely no owner of a clock so silly could be sound on anything else!

All good fun. But the teasing about Jefferson's frailties, early and late, misses what is perhaps the key point—that Jefferson's legacy, admired by all, is elusive for most. It was the product of a privileged moment in history, and, uprooted from the compost of the rich English colonial culture and heritage from which it sprang, Jeffersonianism often has been no match for tribalism, religious zeal, racial hatred, ethnic, linguistic and nationalist rivalries, political ignorance and simple venality. Jefferson had the good fortune to grow up in colonial Virginia, a society where habits of law, responsibility and tolerance (within limits, but rather broad limits for the time) were entrenched, where slavery afforded an economic base for leisure, study and contemplation. In that favored climate, sprigs of the gentry like Thomas Jefferson could dream untroubled dreams of universalizing their legacy. They were wonderful dreams and are vital still. But the Jeffersonian ideals disconnected from their soil and time often wither like the grapevines Jefferson tried to transplant from France to Virginia. All this seems to show that a robust political culture is as vital as ideas to the success of responsible government.

In any case, as Merrill Peterson reminds us, our national heroes usually mean what we want them to mean: an illustration of the truism that history and biography are unstable in part because our aspirations change. Some "new historicists" take this to mean that because it is hard to find the core of character or the truth about an event beneath the clutter of impressions, there is no such core or truth. It is the fashionable new historical heresy, fortunately more appealing to literary scholars than to historians, who know that it is the negation of history to believe that there is no truth apart from subjective imaginings. Somewhere among the many Jeffersons we meet in print and in the monuments he left, there is a real Jefferson, or maybe more than one, but difficult to fix because he was himself a study in self-contradiction. Yet the quest goes on, as it should.

In the Shadow of Lincoln

In *The Jefferson Image in the American Mind* (1960), Merrill Peterson of the University of Virginia patented a new kind of history—the history of a great reputation. Peterson traced the "image" of Jefferson as it evolved and showed that Jefferson had been a mirror in which each age saw itself reflected. He was the touchstone of democratic legitimacy in America.

Thirty-five years later, Peterson added an illuminating companion piece, *Lincoln in American Memory*. There is no dearth of material. There are an estimated sixteen thousand books about Lincoln, who may be the most written-about historical figure since Jesus Christ. From the outset, as Peterson showed, the problem of distinguishing the cultic from the historical has been almost as formidable in Lincoln's case as Albert Schweitzer found it to be when, a century ago, he conducted his "search for the historical Jesus."

The urge to mythologize and even deify the martyred Lincoln was visible from the moment of his death at the hands of John Wilkes Booth and continues unabated. A recent example, though an odd one, is Gore Vidal's huge 1984 novel, *Lincoln,* fact thinly disguised as fiction, history masquerading as invention. And that reverses the usual order.

Vidal has a notoriously mischievous imagination. He is usually hard on national heroes. In writing about Lincoln, however, he is slavishly faithful to the historical record. One reviewer said that Vidal's portrait of the Great Emancipator had "the texture of statuary." Others speculated that Vidal had come to scoff but stayed, as many have done before him, to pray at the shrine. For whatever reason, Vidal carries the fetish of factuality in his novel to remarkable lengths, so much so that the noted Lincoln historian David Donald remarked that he repeatedly checked forgotten details and was surprised at "how much good history" Vidal had put into the story. Even when Vidal takes a liberty—for instance, by putting General McClellan at a party he never attended—he apologizes. Historical scruple can go no further.

But why? If you're going to write so accurately about a president, what is the point of disguising so much diligent legwork as fiction and of sprinkling it with inconsequential invention? If you take pains to find that Lincoln's secretary of state, sometime political rival and would-be mentor, William H. Seward, was a foot shorter, or took snuff, or sneezed loudly into yellow silk handkerchiefs, why treat such nuggets as if you had invented them? The traditional excuse for historical fiction is that it works to enlarge or clarify a mysterious character, or uses historical character as a vehicle for variations on the great themes—vanity or ambition or the like—as in Shakespeare's history plays.

Vidal's novel, again, reverses the usual pattern of Lincoln writing—it is fiction, or at least cultic romance, posing as fact. The Lincoln Memorial remains the monument most visited in Washington, as if the visiting public sensed that there is something behind the veil of myth. And indeed, of all the great presidents, Lincoln remains the most tantalizing challenge to the imagination. He wrote better, reflected more deeply, brooded more bleakly, saw more lucidly into the textures of history, maneuvered more shrewdly, and acted more ruthlessly than anyone else who has ever sat in the office. By comparison, Wilson seems shallow, FDR a Boy

Scout of a political manipulator, Lyndon Johnson a pane of perfect transparency.

Once Lincoln's elaborate and extended state funeral ended, with the mortal remains safely buried in Illinois, the search for the "real" Lincoln, of which Vidal's novel is one of thousands, commenced. By Merrill Peterson's account in *Lincoln in American Memory*, its first phase was primarily reminiscent, a free-for-all marked by bitter rivalries. Would-be chroniclers struggled over the memory of Lincoln, as dedicated apostles might struggle for the mantle of a fallen messiah.

Of all the writers who were to write about him, the first and still in some ways the most influential was Lincoln's twenty-year law partner in Springfield, Illinois, William "Billy" Herndon. Herndon probably saw more of Lincoln before his rise to world fame and martyrdom than anyone other than Mary Todd Lincoln. He exploited that intimacy throughout his remaining years. Herndon was a brilliant prose stylist of a (pre-Freudian) psychoanalytic bent. His own quirks may explain as much as the elusive facts themselves about the Lincoln portrait sketched by his pen. Peterson tells us that Herndon sought truth, and he was at his best on the Lincoln he had uniquely known, the private man. But Herndon's intense distaste for the persistent effort to turn the unorthodox and earthy Lincoln into what H. L. Mencken would later call "a sort of amalgam of John Wesley and the Holy Ghost" tempted Herndon to overcompensate. "Now let it be written in history and on Mr. Lincoln's tomb," Herndon proclaimed in one of his early lectures, "he died an unbeliever." The cultists were shocked, for then as now it was of compelling importance to conventional believers to be assured of Lincoln's religious conventionality.

Herndon would have none of it. From his fertile pen came the famous lecture "Abraham Lincoln, Miss Ann Rutledge, New Salem, Pioneering and the Poem called 'Immortality,' " the locus classicus of the legend of Lincoln's love for Ann Rutledge and of Edgar Lee Masters's haunting poem: "Bloom forever, O Republic, from the dust of my bosom." According to Herndon, Ann and the young Lincoln became secretly engaged during Lincoln's obscure

days in New Salem; her untimely death plunged Lincoln into lasting depression and haunted his allegedly difficult marriage to Mary
Todd. That was the story Herndon told, and it has enjoyed a longer
life than many a well-established fact. Mary Todd Lincoln naturally
disliked it, and its repetition on so many lecture platforms perma-
nently strained her once cordial relationship to Herndon.

In part to offset Herndon's mythologizing influence, Lincoln's
young secretaries, John Nicolay and John Hay, wrote their long,
responsible and often ponderous ten-volume *Abraham Lincoln: A
History* (1890). They drew on their personal recollections and diaries (eight of the ten volumes covered the Civil War years when
they worked closely at the White House with Lincoln). They enjoyed the approval of Lincoln's son, Robert Todd, who was allowed
to vet the work as it went along. Robert Todd Lincoln is known to
have suggested at least one deletion: "a story from [Ward] Lamon's
biography of Lincoln sewing up the eyes of hogs in order to drive
them aboard a flatboat." "A spirit of filiopiety," as Merrill Peterson
calls it, pervades Nicolay and Hay. But it "enshrined the memory
of the Civil War president and transmitted his legend to a new generation with the stamp of authority." Unfortunately, the work did
not sell, although the one-volume abridgment by Nicolay did far
better than the full set.

The first popular Lincoln biography that also pierced the thicken-
ing veils of myth awaited the pen of the hardworking Ida Tarbell,
of "muckraker" and *McClure's Magazine* fame. An assiduous re-
searcher, she recruited assistants in all the scenes of Lincoln's early
life and discovered much new material. *McClure's* was just then, in
the early 1890s, becoming the first of the mass-circulation general
magazines, and Tarbell's investigations of Lincoln became the driving force in an explosion of reader interest and subscriptions. Her
two-volume biography drawn from the same materials became a
runaway best-seller, and so many copies were printed that it is still
to be found in abundance in used-book stores.

Albert Beveridge, fresh from writing about Chief Justice John
Marshall, came next, along with Lord Charnwood's one-volume
life in the "Makers of the 19th Century" series, written during
World War I. Peterson calls Lord Charnwood's book "informative,

thoughtful and discerning" and it was hailed by no less than the *American Historical Review* as an instant classic.

Among the contenders in the middle years were William Barton, father of the advertising mogul and pundit Bruce Barton. Barton left the Christian ministry to set himself up as an arbiter of Lincoln materials. He wrote at length but lacked both Herdon's brilliance of style and Tarbell's ingratiating humanity. Finally, in the twilight of the prehistorical era, came Carl Sandburg's mammoth *The Prairie Years,* a catchall of stories, myths, facts, quotations and nostalgic reminiscences, many of which had been exploded by soberer investigators. Sandburg's subject seemed to be himself as much as Lincoln; his Lincoln biography was derided as "more poetic than much of Sandburg's poetry." Sandburg ran a soberer ship while writing *The War Years,* consulting professional historians and attempting to curb the free-form impulses that later prompted Edmund Wilson to comment that Lincoln had not suffered so at anyone's hands since John Wilkes Booth.

Sandburg's volumes seem to have served as a bridge to the period, commencing in the 1930s, when a new generation of scholars, applying the highest professional standards, dismantled the Lincoln shrine and began to examine their subject more critically. Merrill Peterson dates this transition to J. G. Randall's address to the American Historical Association in 1934 when Randall challenged historians to free themselves "from party and sectional bias . . . [and] the heroic tradition." A succession of distinguished historians—Randall himself, whose four volumes on the presidential Lincoln remain in many ways the best, Richard Current, David Donald, T. Harry Williams and Don Fehrenbacher—began to winnow cult from fact. The paradoxical effect was to show that Lincoln was a greater and deeper figure, certainly a more calculating and effective statesman, than the cult figure. Many of the earlier treatments of Lincoln had, after all, carried undertones of condescension, as if character and genius of the Lincoln dimension could be weighed in the scales of evangelical piety and the "success" and log cabin myths. The newer generation of historians, though interested enough in the old topics of Lincoln's spiritual life, his marriage, his relations with his children, and various tall tales of the railsplitter and backwoods prodigy, were both less credulous and less patronizing. From their writings emerged a clearer picture of Lincoln's political genius, and even his aptitude as a military strategist.

So fascinating a study as Peterson's *Lincoln in American Memory* arouses fresh wonder at the American appetite for historical fictionalizing as a swift route to painless understanding of the great and good. But those who still seek the "real" Abraham Lincoln will learn from Peterson that, in human eyes at least, there is no such figure and probably can't be. As in the case examined by Schweitzer before him, Peterson discovers that the "historical" Lincoln, at least the man we preserve in memory, is elusive. We have only that protean figure who alters with the shifting lights we play upon him, for, like all great men, Lincoln stands always just beyond our reach or touch, receding from the extended hand and eye.

This never has discouraged the pursuers, and probably never will, certainly not those who see in Lincoln's story the possibilities of therapeutic, commercial or promotional advantage. And at least one example of the latter will repay examination.

On Lincoln's birthday in 1980, the United Technologies Company placed a full-page advertisement in the major newspapers. The ad, reviving a standard myth, portrayed Lincoln as an embodiment of chronic bad luck and promised that even the brief contemplation of that luck "will make you feel better." It was one of those familiar blends of cult and conjecture, fact and fantasy, so abundant in popular Lincolniana, of exactly the kind that prompted Richard N. Current to write his entertaining study *The Lincoln Nobody Knows*.

United Technologies' ad writers portray Lincoln as the original hard-luck kid—a "grade-school dropout," debt ridden, unhappily married, political loser, unappreciated orator to "indifferent" audiences, and target of daily press attacks and public contempt. All that notwithstanding, readers were asked to "imagine how many people all over the world have been inspired by this awkward, rumpled, brooding man."

No doubt the principle that misery loves company explains what the admen were driving at. People feeling down on their luck may indeed "feel better" when reminded that destiny has dealt bad hands to great men. Sir Winston Churchill, so often disappointed in his early ambitions as a statesman and strategist, was treated as a "study in failure" by one of his better biographers, Robert Rhodes James. But failure in the raw is seldom inspirational, and I provided the ad with a few corrective footnotes before sending it off to my sixteen-year-old son, then away at school and feeling a bit challenged by fortune.

"He dropped out of grade school": This is a romantic irrelevancy. Lincoln, a man of formidable intellectual power, had less than a year of formal schooling. But while the other frontier youth of Kentucky, Indiana and Illinois were stunning themselves with bad whiskey, he was scouring the neighborhood for books—the Bible, *Pilgrim's Progress*, Grimshaw's *American History*, even Parson Weems's *Life of Washington*—and reading them carefully. His intimate acquaintance with Shakespearean tragedy, no less than with frontier tall tales, impressed colleagues more formally schooled. His mature thought and writing suggest that, if self-taught, he was no "dropout" in the sense in which that term is used now. He attended a reliable university: focused and disciplined private study.

"Took a wife. Unhappy marriage": Lincoln's marriage to Mary Todd of Kentucky in 1842 united two quite different temperaments—hers frothy and explosive, his ironic and forbearing. But, according to biographer Richard Current, "their marriage seems to have been a happy one, their love for each other deep and sincere."

"Ran for House. Lost twice. Ran for Senate. Lost twice": This breathless resume of Lincoln's early political career is silly, to say no more. Donald Fehrenbacher's study of Lincoln's political emergence in the 1850s shows that conventional failures often concealed unconventional successes. Lincoln in fact won a congressional seat (1847–49) and failed to hold it only because he soon established himself in the House as an independent spirit, challenging President Polk's disingenuous justification of the Mexican War. The young Whig's skeptical stance cost him reelection in Illinois. But it laid the foundation for his later emergence as a champion of "free soil" sentiment, an important reminder that politicians do not always advance their fortunes by watering down their convictions.

His campaign for a U. S. Senate seat against Stephen A. Douglas in 1858 became the occasion of the famous debates and strengthened Lincoln's preeminent national standing in the Whig-Republican antislavery cause. It led to a presidential nomination two years later. Few races for the Senate were ever more beneficially lost.

"Delivered speech that became classic. Audience indifferent": Those who heard Lincoln at Gettysburg, the more discerning members of the audience at any rate, quickly recognized the majesty of his remarks. Edward Everett, the featured speaker, handsomely acknowledged the superiority of Lincoln's brief oration over his own lengthier and more conventional address. Many others agreed and said so at the time.

"Attacked daily by the press and despised by half the country": True, alas. But Lincoln wisely ignored the newspapers and took his bearings from a sure intuition of the deeper tides. To be attacked daily in the press and to be despised by half the country has been the lot of many other presidents with a solid claim to historical attention, including Jefferson, Truman and Franklin D. Roosevelt. It may be heartening to reflect that great figures are often stalled by adversity, but the loopholes in the United Technologies ad warn of the deceptiveness of appearances and the poverty of mere chronologies. In the great historical struggles, the pattern beneath the visible evidence may be elusive and often misleading in the short term. That is the sum, indeed, of what Lincoln, man and myth, teaches us about history, early and late.

Who Was Thaddeus Stevens?

IT IS BEYOND IMAGINING what old Thaddeus Stevens might have said as he lay dying in August 1868 had he foreseen that, within little more than a century, the daughter of a Georgia-born president would attend a Washington, D. C., elementary school named in his honor. Something sarcastic, perhaps. An appreciation of the small ironies of history was not among his virtues, and even less so, probably, if a small irony would link him with the descendents of "proud traitors."

The civil rights revolution in our time—the "second reconstruction," as our greatest southern historian, C. Vann Woodward, has called it—has revived an appreciation of Stevens's virtues. For earlier students of American history, southerners anyway, his faults were such as to rank him only slightly below John Wilkes Booth as a spoiler of national reconciliation after the Civil War. In designing revenge upon the defeated South, he made his name as the extremist of extremists. He was the foremost exponent of the view that in seceding, the Confederate states had committed suicide and forfeited statehood. In this, of course, he and other congressional "rad-icals" sharply differed with Abraham Lincoln, who throughout the war treated secession as a domestic rebellion committed by individ-uals. Stevens also instigated the impeachment of President Andrew Johnson. The judgment of the *Dictionary of American Biography* is unsparing: "An intense partisan, his career was marred by a harsh and vindictive temper which in his last years made him frankly vengeful toward the South. His policy aroused fierce resentment, accentuated racial antagonism, cemented the Solid South, and post-poned for many decades any true solution of the race problem. Had tolerance been added to his character, he might have been a brilliant instead of a sinister figure in American history."

That was the received view of Stevens as recently as thirty years ago, certainly earlier, and it has some elements of historical carica-ture. Rehabilitation began to set in when the young Amy Carter enrolled in 1977 at Thaddeus Stevens Elementary School in Wash-ington, with her father's arrival at the White House. The historian Eric Foner, a leading authority on the Reconstruction period, polled his American history class at Princeton. To his dismay, he reported in the *New York Times*, "not a single student" knew who Stevens was. Foner set out to remedy their ignorance and that of *Times* readers. Having once "symbolized Northern malice, revenge and irrational hatred of the South," Stevens, Foner believes, has come to symbolize something more wholesome: the demand for racial and political equality.

"What is most striking," writes Foner, "is how thoroughly tradi-tional his beliefs actually were." Stevens believed in racial equality, free schools, the Declaration of Independence, and the yeoman farmer; what could be so bad about that? As for Stevens's speeches, they "could have been written by Jefferson."

Stevens must have his due as an early prophet of racial equality. But Foner's rehabilitation illustrates the hazard of reading present political sentiments into the past. In the process of rehabilitation, Foner irons too many angles out of the historic Stevens. It is the "horrible old man" portrait reversed, the sarcastic, caustic, club-footed hypocrite beatified. But sanctity sits no more credibly on Thaddeus Stevens than does villainy.

Stevens was no traditionalist. He was, first and last, a "radical" Republican (and before that a so-called "conscience Whig," who opposed political compromise with fugitive slave laws and who defended runaway slaves without charge). He assailed every tradition, good or bad, that contradicted his own notions of political virtue. The French statesmen Georges Clemenceau, in a history of the Reconstruction period that he wrote as a journalist and overseas observer many years before he became the World War I premier of France, pronounced him the "Robespierre" of the "radical reconstruction." Since Stevens was a powerful and theatrical speechmaker, it was sometimes hard to winnow the belief from the bombast. In a typically purple speech to the House of Representatives in December 1865, Stevens demanded that the South be considered to have reverted to territorial status, there to "eat the fruit of foul rebellion. . . . These fallen rebels cannot at their option reenter the heaven which they have disturbed . . . These extinct states . . . now have no more existence than the revolted cities of Latium whose people were colonized and their property confiscated and their rights of citizenship withdrawn by conquering and avenging Rome."

More moderate men, no less keen than Stevens to consolidate the lessons of a bitter war, saw the issue of reconstruction rather differently. If secession was illegal, as the Republicans claimed, how could the rebel states have lost their statehood or forfeited rights of citizenship because some thousands of individuals had participated in rebellion? If the Union had been "indissoluble," as Lincoln claimed, how could it have been dissolved? Stevens was having none of this. His view of reconstruction was uncompromising. Every resident of the seceded states, guilty or not of overt acts of rebellion, would become stateless. Planters' lands would be confiscated and redistributed. The "extinct" states might later be readmitted to the Union, but only on terms guaranteeing the domination of the Republican Party. That was the original intent, apparently, of an unused section of the Fourteenth Amendment that provides for the reduction of southern representation in the House, in proportion to any disfranchisement of former slaves. Had Congress enforced it, as it clearly had the power to do, the long decades of

exclusion of blacks from politics would have been inconceivable—
let that much be said for Stevens. If Andrew Johnson should attempt to stand in the way of Stevens's reconstruction design, he
must be tried on flimsy impeachment charges and very nearly
ousted—Stevens was a ringleader of the Johnson impeachment.
Congressional will would be put beyond presidential check or challenge.

Stevens's role in the Johnson impeachment fares little better from
a constitutional standpoint than some of his ideas about reconstruction. Every schoolboy knows, or used to know, the story of the
unsuccessful Johnson impeachment—how Johnson was acquitted
by a single vote in the Senate. Far less is remembered about the
alleged presidential offense that roused Stevens and his allies to im-
peach Johnson. It was his violation of a dubious statute (later repu-
diated by the Supreme Court), the so-called Tenure of Office Act.
Congress sought to tie Johnson's hands by making presidential subordinates—even cabinet officers—accountable to the Senate by pro-
viding that they could be removed only with its consent. When
Johnson fired Secretary of War Edwin Stanton, the radical Republicans' mole in his inner circle, the House shouted through impeachment charges in a matter of hours. The assumption was that under
the Tenure of Office Act, Stanton could not be removed without
the Senate's permission. But Lincoln, not Johnson, had appointed
Stanton in the first place, and it was unclear that the act, even in its
own terms, was binding. This flawed legislation remained on the
books for a long time, unenforced, but the Taft Supreme Court
established its unconstitutionality in 1927 when, in *Myers* v. *U.S.*,
the Court said that the presidential power to discharge subordinates
is an essential corollary of the duty to "take care that the laws be
faithfully executed." The removal power could not be diluted by
Congress, a view that early congresses had shared with the framers.

Stevens excused his revolutionary measures—and they were no
less than that—by citing the Declaration of Independence, even
though a member of the infamous "slavocracy" had written it and
many who were not believers in mass democracy had signed it.
Stevens's means were as revolutionary as some of his goals were

admirable, and, in a constitutional system, means are never separable from ends, even in wartime.

Stevens was the prototype of a familiar figure in American politics, a man of revolutionary temperament masquerading as a democrat, a reformer prepared to bend the Constitution to achieve his ends, an avenger whose approach to political action invariably alienates moderate opinion and invites reaction, the politician who rewrites the historical evidence to suit his immediate purposes. Stevens alone can't fairly be blamed for the failure of Reconstruction, but his ferocity and intemperance had a lot to do with the failure.

When I expressed this view of Stevens in a column in the *Washington Star* in response to Eric Foner in 1977, my correspondents, including Foner himself, protested that I had drawn a one-sided portrait of Stevens. The impenitent and obstructionist attitudes of the southern states, and their cynical and exploitative treatment of the freed slaves, was sufficient provocation for the "radicals." One letter writer said that I had given in to "the Southern sentimentalists." Another wrote that "when a man long dead and almost forgotten is subjected to personal abuse . . . I am justified in suspecting the motives of his detractors." I had not, he suggested, forgiven Stevens for being "an implacable opponent of slavery."

Eric Foner's attempt to crown Stevens as a martyr to all that was good and prophetic might have led me to stumble, as he had, into historical caricature. I certainly had no intention of reviving a discredited school of thought about Reconstruction. The Lord Macaulay of that earlier school was Claude G. Bowers, whose seductively readable book, *The Tragic Era,* takes the same harsh line on Stevens—"as much a revolutionist," Bowers says, "as Marat in his tub. Had he lived in France in the days of the Terror, he would have pushed one of the Triumvirate desperately for his place, have risen rapidly to the top through his genius and will, and probably have died by the guillotine with a sardonic smile upon his face."

Much the same view of the Civil War and Reconstruction was taken by Bowers's contemporary, the historian Charles A. Beard, who viewed our "second revolution" as primarily the violent overthrow of the farmer-planter class by budding capitalists and the abolition of slavery as a stupendous "sequestration" of landed wealth. Beard discovered money-power conspiracy on the slightest evidence. In *The Rise of American Civilization,* Beard wrote that "at bottom the so-called Civil War . . . was a social war, ending in the unquestioned establishment of a new power in the government, making vast changes in the arrangement of classes, in the accumulation and distribution of wealth, in the course of industrial development and in the Constitution."

To anyone who grew up in the South a few decades ago, and even to many who didn't, this view of the Civil War and—especially—Reconstruction was historical mother's milk. Recent historians have demonstrated that in its one-sidedness it was closer to historical eyewash. The antagonisms that led to "radical" Reconstruction were not unprovoked. The extremism of Stevens and his allies must be understood in the light of the personality and tactics of Andrew Johnson, a well-meaning but limited man who thought of himself as the last defender of the Constitution, but whose intemperate and ineffectual resistance to congressional views merely fanned extremism. Johnson, a man of monumental political ineptitude, lacked the skill to provide a rallying point for moderate opinion. He believed that his congressional critics were indistinguishable from the "traitors" he had opposed as a beleaguered unionist in Tennessee; in this he was tragically wrong. The constitutional conflict between Johnson and the congressional "radicals," including Stevens, cannot be understood as mere political melodrama. Johnson and Stevens alike shared an obsessive hatred of the southern ruling class, and it led both of them astray. But there were real issues at stake in the debate over Reconstruction, and, after so much sacrifice of life, it was understandably infuriating to strong unionists to think that all that blood had been spent for nought.

As the controversy over Stevens unfolded, I began to realize that Eric Foner was probably right in guessing that few Americans would recall who Stevens was. When I recalled Beard's judgment, and the kindred view of Claude Bowers, I had not yet read a book that explains a great deal about the climate in which their views were shaped.

That book is Brooks Adams's fascinating venture in metahistory,

The Law of Civilization and Decay. A 1955 reissue of Adams's book has a lengthy and admiring prefatory essay by Beard, and no wonder. Adams's argument is that Western history is the tale of a continuing contest between capitalism (and "economic man," *Homo economicus*) on the one hand, and a landed interest of planters and farmers, soldiers, poets, clergy and other men of imagination on the other. The latter, according to Brooks Adams, are marked by an unworldly attachment to values other than the cash nexus. The Adams thesis provides a revealing clue to what Beard, Bowers, and other progressives thought had befallen the United States during its "second revolution." In their eyes, the moral drama of slavery, the centerpiece today of most writing about the causes and results of the Civil War, was secondary to the struggle of aggrandizing capitalists against the planter interest. "Law," writes Adams in a typical passage, "is merely the expression of the will of the strongest for the time being, and therefore laws have no fixity but shift from generation to generation. When the imagination is vivid and police weak, emotional or ecclesiastical law prevails. As competition sharpens, and the movement of society accelerates, religious ritual is supplanted by civil codes for the enforcement of contracts and the protection of the creditor class."

Like his more eminent historian brother, Henry, Brooks Adams was bedazzled by the idea of a "scientific" history—history whose cycles could be explained and even predicted by laws modeled on those of the exciting new nineteenth-century sciences of Darwinism and thermodynamics. Historians think less well of that kind of history today, for it is clear that, in the first place, the "laws" of natural science are less deterministic than they seemed to intelligent observers a century ago, and that, in the second place, history can't be made obedient to fixed laws without substantial manipulation of evidence. Beard and Bowers, like the Adamses, were repelled by the political extremism and rapacity of the Republican "radicals" and by the relaxed public morality of the Gilded Age. Notwithstanding their devotion to the Union cause—and their father's critical role as Lincoln's minister to London during the Civil War—they became conservatives and Democrats. In Thaddeus Stevens, we see epitomized the mentality at which the sting of *The Law of Civilization and Decay* is aimed.

The "How's the President Doing" Question

૭

THE LATE HEDLEY DONOVAN, Henry Luce's successor as editor in chief of the Time-Life publications, was a model of journalistic sobriety and intellectual curiosity whom I had the pleasure of knowing in his later years. Hedley liked to convene editorial luncheons in the Time-Life Building's executive dining suite above the clouds in New York and, over good food and drink, conduct informal seminars on presidential performance—the "how's the president doing question," as he called it.

One day in 1978, I had flown up from Washington for such an occasion. I was then editing the editorial page of the *Washington Star*, which Time, Inc. had just bought. Hedley invited me to lead off a discussion of the state of the Carter presidency. How was Carter doing? In all candor, I might have asked: "Compared to whom? And when?" But such questions would have been uncollegial, and certainly unjournalistic. So I did my best. But it is very hard to say how a president is "doing" except with reference to the fickle standards journalists establish when they're eager for copy.

When he left the Time-Life editorship, Donovan went to work as a special assistant to Jimmy Carter and later wrote a good book about recent presidencies. At the time, I sent him a rather solemn letter taking up the question he had asked about Carter months earlier, writing at some length about what seemed to me to be troubling the administration. Obviously, my earlier modesty in making instant judgments had faded. Carter was in trouble, as the 1980 election was to prove. A thumping inflation and an interest-rate spike had been generated by the shutdown of the Iranian oil fields and rising world oil prices—the second "oil shock" of the 1970s, and, in dollar terms, far more severe in its impact than the first in 1973. Added to that was the kidnaping of American diplomats at the Teheran embassy and Carter's insistence (in which he was joined by the press) on making their detention the centerpiece of the news and a consuming national preoccupation, more satisfying than not to their captors. Carter's misfortune might move one to wonder just how much presidential destiny is imposed by chance events, beyond a president's power to control. Even Lincoln, who isn't ordinarily seen as a "weak" president, "confessed" that he had often been more controlled by events than in control of them.

The one twentieth-century president whose greatness has never seriously been questioned is Franklin D. Roosevelt. But when his kinsman Joseph Alsop, the Washington columnist, wrote his brilliant memoir *FDR: A Centennial Remembrance* in 1982, misconceptions about Roosevelt abounded. Alsop was highly qualified to attempt a restoration. He was cousins with both the Republican Oyster Bay and Democratic Hyde Park branches of the Roosevelt family and was on friendly personal terms with FDR. From family talk, he knew that no one had detected in the younger FDR the mettle of a future president. The girls in the family had called him "the feather duster," suggesting lightness. Alsop's mother, an assertive Connecticut Republican, thought FDR looked like the wimpish young fop on gift handkerchief boxes of her day. The shaping of a great president out of the young "feather duster" remains a mystery that Joe Alsop, as he told me, pondered for years. It was obvious that the sudden attack of polio that crippled Roosevelt as a young man in the early 1920s, as well as his baffled love affair with the beautiful Lucy Mercer, had a maturing effect. Both are twice-told tales, to which Alsop added uniquely informed judgments.

For earlier generations, FDR was the buoyant leader who conquered the Great Depression and the war leader who joined with Winston Churchill to save democracy from Hitler and Tojo. Alsop believes that any president who prevails in two supreme crises necessarily ranks among the handful of great ones. FDR restored hope to a demoralized nation and, by timely measures, "included the excluded" in the bounty of everyday life. Some of the old WASP ruling class to which Alsop as well as Franklin Roosevelt belonged felt betrayed by the latter transformation, his patronage of minorities and laboring people, and their resentment fed the ugly phenomenon of Roosevelt-hating. But the contemporary forms of Roosevelt-hating have more recently given way to bizarre styles of detraction, typified by the curious view of his successor, Ronald Reagan, that the New Deal was inspired by Benito Mussolini's fascist movement.

The emergence of that curious idea, two years before Alsop's centennial memoir appeared, followed an essentially journalistic chronology. It originated in an article in the *Wall Street Journal* by an economist, Prof. Melvyn Krauss of New York University. Krauss defended Ronald Reagan's choice of Mussolini as the intellectual father of the New Deal, saying that it "should at least merit him a good mark on economic history." But the suggestion that strained comparisons between the "corporativism" of Italian fascism and the New Deal's National Industrial Recovery Act (NIRA) make fascism "the basis of the New Deal" is F-grade history. There was a voguish enthusiasm for Mussolini in the depression years. "For a time," writes Ronald Steel in his biography of Walter Lippmann, "Mussolini enjoyed the virtually unanimous support of the American press. . . . Among the major magazines, *Harper's* and *The Atlantic* stood in lonely opposition."

Does that mean that the architects of the NIRA were under Mussolini's influence also, or that the National Recovery Administration operated upon fascist principles, or that the NIRA was the paradigmatic New Deal measure? The NIRA was a potpourri of reformist nostrums, encouraging cooperation between management and labor. Everyone from the U. S. Chamber of Commerce to the American Federation of Labor had a hand in concocting the NRA legislation. The Supreme Court finally overturned NRA, not because it embodied antidemocratic ideas but because it delegated excessive legislative power to the president. Krauss was far off in suggesting that "the corporate state constituted the economic basis of . . . the New Deal and the European welfare state," an assertion that scants American progressivism, Fabian socialism in Britain and even Otto von Bismarck's social insurance program in nineteenth-century Germany. How did Krauss reach these unhistorical conclusions? By argument from analogy. Analogical argument can be fruitful in the comparative study of political and economic institutions, but it is of little value in sorting out historical causes and antecedents. For the historian, similarities may or may not suggest imitation. The documented precedent, the lineage of an idea or policy, is primary. The pseudohistorian supposes that parallels are identical with causes, clearly a fallacy, since by analogy the historical sophist can demonstrate almost any bogus historical connection, from the "Marxist" origins of the American income tax to the "fascist" inspiration of the New Deal.

Joe Alsop demonstrates in his memoir that FDR was no sort of ideologue, and certainly no imitation Mussolini. But the neglect of history makes Americans vulnerable these days to historical vandalism that is no less disfiguring for being performed with pen and ink than a torch or a bomb. Alsop's memoir was not only a sound corrective; it was a primer on successful presidencies. FDR, as Alsop shows, was a political animal and an unsurpassed educator of public sentiment. He knew the art of using subordinates who imagined that they were using him. "The plain truth," writes Alsop, "is that Roosevelt was perfectly ready to follow a political course that would have broken a snake's back if that course finally took him where he wanted to be." The serpentine course occasionally played FDR false, Alsop believes, as when he tried to justify his 1937 attempt to pack the Supreme Court with new justices sympathetic to his program by claiming that the Court was overworked. That phony argument played into the hands of a master judicial politician, Chief Justice Charles Evans Hughes, who demolished it with facts and figures in congressional testimony. Alsop believes that a more candid confession of FDR's aims would have yielded better results, at lower political cost. But his evaluation of Roosevelt is a reminder that a firm grasp of presidential character and goals may take years to emerge.

Dwight D. Eisenhower's presidential reputation has been less stable than FDR's since he left the White House in 1961. But its continuing ascent is an awkward subject for journalists who underestimated him in office. Even historians sometimes make brash short-term appraisals—as when fifty noted American historians dismissed Eisenhower as a "near failure" not long after he left office. The steady recovery of Eisenhower's postpresidential reputation (his reputation as a soldier had never been in question) constitutes a salutary warning against premature evaluations of any presidency. And after reading Steven Ambrose's massive book *Eisenhower the President* (1984), we may well wonder how sound our information about any sitting president really is.

Ambrose lets some contemporary judgments stand. He shares the view, widespread in the 1950s, that Eisenhower should have rebuked Sen. Joe McCarthy more sharply, and not permitted his demagoguery on the issue of Communist penetration of American government to become a blot on the era. New documents available to Ambrose—notably the diaries of Gen. Andrew Goodpaster—show that Eisenhower shrank from "getting down into the gutter" with McCarthy for fear that the collision would divide the country and lower the prestige of the presidency, which it was among his majors to "restore." (He took the rather condescending view that Harry S Truman had been an "undignified" occupant of the office.)

Ambrose also echoes the contemporary complaint that by declining to endorse the Supreme Court's 1954 decision on school segregation, Eisenhower gave heart to obstructionists. Speaking of the crisis provoked by Arkansas Gov. Orval Faubus's defiance of a court order to integrate Central High School in Little Rock, he writes: "The upshot of [Eisenhower's] conflicting emotions and statements was confusion, which allowed the segregationists to convince themselves that the president would never act." Faubus and his lawless followers were wrong; Eisenhower would not tolerate lawlessness. Yet he hung back from endorsing the *Brown* decision. The truth was that he shared the conventional southern wisdom that it would be folly to push ahead with speedy integration.

These two matters aside, however, Ambrose's book is celebratory, often a bit giddily so. It is clear now that Eisenhower was a far better-informed and focused president than he occasionally seemed. But a presidency must be judged by accomplishments as well as intentions, and Ike's good intentions were not always rewarded. He did end the Korean War, though not, as rumor later had it, by threatening to use atomic weapons against China. He kept the United States out of the nasty postcolonial war in Indochina (which his successors would stumble into) by laying down preconditions of intervention, including joint participation by the British, that he knew would not be met. By the exercise of masterly ambiguity, he contained the trivial but dangerous confrontation with China in the Straits of Formosa, where the periodic shelling of the islands of Quemoy and Matsu from the mainland kept a minor war scare simmering through much of the 1950s. Ambrose shows that Eisenhower's successes in these and other matters were the result of adroit and calculated exercises of political skill and good judgment.

Ambrose worked on his biography for twenty years, and it would be fanciful to think that its focus was shaped by current trends. Yet later awareness of Eisenhower's successes was undoubtedly sharpened by events of the Reagan years. Eisenhower had passionately believed that it would be self-defeating to inflate the economy by exorbitant deficit financing and an undiscriminating arms buildup. He drew upon his personal authority as an old soldier and military administrator to contain Pentagon excesses that, under his successors, especially Reagan, got ruinously out of hand. Ambrose shows how, amid the hysteria generated by the launching of the first Russian space satellite, Sputnik, in 1957, Eisenhower also fended off the argument that the United States was threatened by a "missile gap"—that is, potential Russian strategic superiority. Thanks to the still secret U-2 surveillance, he knew that the United States was well ahead of the Soviet Union in the counters of strategic power.

The story of the Eisenhower presidency is perhaps more complex than Ambrose allows. It was, for instance, politically sterile, in the sense that Ike failed to exploit his great personal popularity by changing the fundamental nature of the Republican Party or "modernizing" it as he fervently wished to do. The control of Congress by the Democrats through most of his two terms didn't especially bother him, since the Democrats (especially the southerners) seemed to him more responsible and serious about the issues, especially foreign policy issues, than the troglodytes of his own party. He fantasized about persuading Frank Lausche, governor of Ohio and a moderate Democrat, to run with him in 1956. He tried to persuade another Democrat, his second-term secretary of the treasury, Robert Anderson, to seek the presidency. All these projects failed, and his political disappointments help explain why the eastern establishment Republicanism of which his candidacy was the last triumph has given way to the Reagan Republicanism of the Sun Belt.

And then there is Richard M. Nixon. There is, of course, no shortage of partisan judgments; the historical ones are more difficult. We can already see more clearly than when the Nixon impeachment case was pending that he and his blundering henchmen did not invent political espionage or the partisan use of the FBI. More recent inquiries have not uncovered abuses so grave as those perpetrated by the so-called Plumbers Unit, an extralegal and secret task force underwritten by campaign funds and charged with political espionage directed from the White House. This was much the gravest infraction of custom and law in the modern presidency up to that time. But there is modest force in the contention of Nixon's defenders that his crimes differed from those of predecessors only in degree, not principle, and in that he was caught. A more interesting question, perhaps, is why he alone was caught. Because an alert night watchman in the Watergate office building noticed that the doors to the Democratic National Committee headquarters had been taped open one July evening? Or because attempted bribery failed to buy the silence of the burglars who had broken into it? This is Cleopatra's Nose history, and great events rarely pivot on details so minute.

The historical point is that Richard Nixon strained even accepted presidential custom, and could not distinguish clearly between expedients and precedents. Did Franklin D. Roosevelt secretly order U. S. Navy destroyers to aid British convoys well beyond the limits of the neutrality acts in the North Atlantic in the months before World War II? He did; so Nixon assumed license to fight a secret war in Cambodia. Did other presidents occasionally impound appropriated funds? They did; so Nixon attempted to expand impoundment into a weapon for challenging congressional policy, as well as excessive spending. Did Lyndon Johnson spy on Barry Goldwater during the 1964 presidential campaign? Perhaps; so Nixon would set up a secret White House spy-and-burglary corps. Nixon failed to sense, in time, that a drastic reaction had set in against aggressive presidencies, and that this reaction had sharply lowered tolerance for quasi-legal activities even as he tested new limits of presidential discretion and made extravagant constitutional claims. Of the authorization of certain "national security" wiretaps, he went so far as to say that "if a president orders it, it isn't illegal," as if mere presidential will could confer legality on doubtful exercises of power. He was, in fact, a James I of a president, treating as settled precedent what his more cautious predecessors treated as the most unusual expedient.

Nixon's Achilles' heel, apart from paranoia, was a lawyerly bent of a plodding and literal-minded kind. He was the first lawyer-president of the postwar era, and was prone to offer assertive legalistic briefs for every questionable act. This became the background for his fall, but it needed a precipitating event, and that was the attempt to brazen his way through the Watergate scandal by bribery, deception and coverup. What if Nixon, in June 1972, had decided to come clean—to follow what his counselor John Ehrlichman was later to call the "hang-out route"? It would have been a desperate gamble. There would have been a mighty uproar, and it might well have sunk his campaign for reelection. But then, it just might have worked—assuming, of course, that Nixon himself was not complicit in the original burglary of the Democratic National Committee headquarters and knew nothing of it before June 17, 1972. Viewed in hindsight, the coverup strategy was much riskier than an immediate confession would have been. Nixon laid a trap for himself and, once caught in it, had nowhere to go but out.

History's ultimate judgment on Nixon's crimes may be as unstable as our own, but will rest on answers to questions we now can only ask and answer provisionally: was he part of—or a radical departure from—a progressive twentieth-century trend, fed by two world wars and by the rise of the national security state during the long contest with the Soviet Union, that dragged the presidency into a shadowy world of quasi-legality? Will time sanction the extreme fears of public disorder and peril abroad from which this illegality arose? We have come now to the end of the cold war whose creature, exploiter and peacemaker (all at different stages and moods) Richard Nixon was. That will give us distance and perspective in time but not yet.

Was Ronald W. Reagan "the most successful president since Franklin D. Roosevelt"? Or was he "a lazy, ignorant president pursuing errant policies . . . a slothful ignoramus who inspired a decade of greed and self-indulgence"? The columnists Rowland Evans and Robert Novak posed that either/or question about the Reagan presidency a few years after it ended in a 1987 column captioned "Deconstructing Reagan." They worried that the second *image* (a word advisedly used in journalism purporting to assess presidencies) was quickly overtaking the first, unresisted even by the former president's admirers. They discovered symptoms of this wild swing of the historical weather vane, this "deconstructed image," in a number of events and portraits—Kitty Kelly's "trash biography" of Nancy Reagan, with its tales of petticoat influence at the White House, for instance, and in the allegations of a former National Security Council military aide that the Reagan campaign in 1980 may have made a secret bargain with the Iranians to delay the release of American diplomatic hostages in Teheran until after election day.

Few presidencies but the very best and the very worst are likely to be judged under such extreme either/or polarities. Reagan seems unlikely to occupy either the topmost or bottommost rung of presidential reputation. As was the case when he was in office, Reagan's reputation rests on his gift for creating inspirational illusion. It is perhaps a useful presidential talent but a dangerous one. No recent president, none since FDR anyway, has played the head of state's role more splendidly. For Reagan it was indeed "the role of a lifetime," in the words of his biographer Lou Cannon. But no president since Warren G. Harding so frequently seemed lax in command and in his control over subordinates. The marine barracks bombing in Lebanon, the Iran-Contra scandal (the most serious assault on constitutional regularity in the conduct of foreign policy of the postwar era), the infamously costly savings and loan debacle, the wholesale theft of public funds at the Department of Housing and Urban Development—these and other episodes of the Reagan years seemed to proceed almost independently of Reagan himself. He enjoyed a remarkable immunity to the usual political consequences, although he was surely accountable for them. They are likely to weigh heavily in the negative column as the historical assessment proceeds.

Yet it is odd to suggest, as Evans and Novak did, that "academic historians have rushed to judgment to flunk Reagan as quickly as they did Harry Truman and Dwight Eisenhower." An odd comparison. The Truman presidency has not yet been the subject of a major academic study, and Truman's presidential reputation has been steadily rising for decades. Two full-length studies, both by journalists (Robert Donovan and the late Cabell Phillips) are affectionate and admiring. Eisenhower, whose stock did plunge for a time, has benefited from the attentions of "academic historians." (I noted Stephen Ambrose's biography above.) And in a major revisionist study, Prof. Fred Greenstein of Princeton has argued that Eisenhower conducted a subtle "hidden-hand presidency" and was far more completely in control than he seemed.

Ronald Reagan's turn to be put in perspective will come, and two hard questions about his presidency are certain: will the threefold increase in the national debt (and accordingly in interest burdens) which was the direct consequence of his fiscal policies be viewed as symptomatic of a general failure of political will, encompassing all contemporaneous presidencies and both political branches? Or will it be seen as a peculiar result of Reagan's deep tax-cutting policies and "Reaganomics"? And what will be the ultimate effects on the American economy?

Will the end of the cold war look like the subsidence of a rivalry instigated by Soviet aggression, and ended by internal reforms and changes of outlook, combined with the happy accident of Mikhail Gorbachev? Or will it be seen as a result to which Reagan's costly defense buildup drove the Russians by making the cost of armed rivalry prohibitive? The Soviet archives should be useful here. These and other material questions will hardly be settled by trash biographers like Kitty Kelly, or tittle-tattle about Nancy Reagan's consultation of astrologers, or even by excellent near-term assessments by Gary Wills and Lou Cannon. Edmund Morris, the prizewinning biographer of Theodore Roosevelt, was given uninhibited access to the Reagan White House, and his book is eagerly awaited. But none of these books, perhaps not even Morris's, will set the mold of Reagan's presidential reputation. It will depend on events and perspectives to come, interpreted by historians now in kneepants or even unborn. And, as J. P. Morgan said of the stock market, it will fluctuate.

If I were asked Hedley Donovan's probing question about William Jefferson Clinton, my first instinct, as usual, would be to declare it premature. My second would be to confess a personal interest that may impair journalistic and historical judgment alike. I am what has come to be called an "FOB," a friend of Bill's, though distinctly of the second or third tier in that vast network.

I first heard Clinton's name from his Oxford classmate Strobe Talbott, who asked me one day in 1978 whether I knew of him. "He's the new governor of Arkansas," Talbott said, "and a major political talent. Keep your eye on him." Talbott's was useful and prophetic advice—and shortly after Clinton's election in 1992 Talbott told me that while he wished to avoid immodesty, he *thought* he had believed in their Oxford days that Clinton would someday be president.

I meanwhile drifted into Clinton's magnetic field in 1987, when he and I, together with our wives, attended a conference of state, county and local officials, American and Italian, in Florence. It was a good week of talk, conviviality and sight-seeing. As chairman of the National Governors Conference, Clinton became the spokesman for the Americans and an engaging one. Our own best visit occurred one evening at a hill town overlooking Florence. We had a long talk over dinner about the pending nomination of Robert Bork to the Supreme Court. Clinton was under pressure to testify against Bork, but was reluctant to do so since he had taken constitutional law from Bork at Yale and felt some personal regard for the man if not for his judicial views. Clinton later opposed Bork's confirmation, but in a letter to the Senate Judiciary Committee rather than in personal testimony. It was not the first, or only, instance of Clinton's celebrated propensity for splitting differences and smoothing rough edges that might bruise someone else's feelings. The instinct is not false, for Clinton is a genuinely warm and friendly man whose attractiveness is rooted in a keen personal interest in others. The Florence meeting ripened into friendship as we continued to see the Clintons at various gatherings at Hilton Head and in Washington. When he was on the verge of announcing for president in late 1991, I wrote what he and I both remember as the first strong newspaper endorsement of his candidacy.

Like so many other early admirers, I have come to feel that there is something of a mismatch between Bill Clinton's manifest gifts—his generosity of temperament, his intelligence, his keen interest in the fine detail of public issues, his zest for political play, his idealism—and the more prosaic demands of the post–cold war presidency. I was among those who thought in 1992 that Clinton, with his southern "New Democrat" credentials, would be just the remedy for a Democratic Party that had too long deferred to its more radical factions and made itself chronically unelectable. His reinforcement of those moderating qualities with the choice of Al Gore as his running mate seemed inspired. I genuinely expected Clinton to restructure the Democratic coalition, to subdue its single-issue zealots, and with luck to become the FDR of the new age. But the health care fiasco—his attempt to interest Congress and the public

in a sweeping redesign of the nation's health insurance system—
followed by the loss of Congress in 1994 to Republican majorities
in both chambers for the first time since the Eisenhower era, swept
all early bets from the table.

In the fullness of time, historians may say that the latter rebuke,
raising to prominence an abrasive Republican Speaker, Newt
Gingrich, was a political godsend to Clinton. It unshackled him
from the more importunate factions of his own party and positioned him to do what he enjoys far more than the tedious disci-
plines of governance: campaigning against identifiable foes.

From the seating of the new Republican Congress in January
1995, Clinton campaigned with a touch of genius, exploiting every
Republican blunder. But there was a price. As he listened more
and more to his political Svengali, Dick Morris, a consultant whose
political interests were exclusively tactical, Clinton's presidency
took on an appearance of political pointillism. A Seurat of minor
issues, Clinton brushed in a bewildering variety of minute dots and
daubs of policy, many of which seemed distinctly subpresidential,
including a statement in favor of uniforms in the public schools.
The danger, historically speaking, was that these micromanaged
proposals would never add up to a picture. If Clinton's predecessor,
George Bush, had confessed to being, in his own words, deficient
in "the vision thing," Clinton too seemed to be tempted on occasion by the same trap of pragmatism and triviality.

Perhaps he was not unaware of the danger, for, just before the
1996 Democratic National Convention in Chicago, in which Clinton was nominated for a second term, it was reported that Clinton
and his strategist Morris had sat down one day at the White House
to discuss the scale of his presidential aspirations. They were said
to have agreed that in the absence of monumental challenges (depression, war, nuclear terror, etc.) Clinton's realistic prospect was
to aspire to the standing of a president of the "second rung." It
seems a realistic goal.

Certainly his admirers would like to see Bill Clinton leave a mark
on the office worthy of his political talents. But Clinton's destiny as
president has thus far been confined by the circumstances that made
him electable. Once the collapse of the Berlin Wall made it clear

that the division of Germany and Europe was no longer sustainable, Bush and Mikhail Gorbachev negotiated a civil conclusion to the cold war. Bush and Gorbachev promptly suffered similar fates, both of them unceremoniously discarded in a manner reminiscent of the British electorate's curt dismissal of Winston Churchill in the 1945 elections, after the exertions of World War II. For the first time in the forty-year cold war era, American voters apparently felt that they could take a chance on a youthful president who had avoided military service and whose credentials in foreign policy were modest. For the first time in nearly half a century—really, for the first time since it became ominously clear in the autumn of 1949 that the Russians had obtained atomic weapons—it mattered significantly less whose finger was to be on the nuclear trigger. But there was a corollary deflation of the importance of presidential leadership. In the flattened domestic and international terrain, lacking exhilarating peaks and darker valleys, heroic issues had vanished or been muted. And, as the foregoing examples show, the history of great presidencies has been a history of big challenges met and overcome.

Bill Clinton has weathered the 1996 challenge and embarked with renewed hope on a second term after a first term of mixed successes and failures, occasionally more notable for miscalculations than for triumphs. He certainly miscalculated the nation's willingness to undertake a vastly complex overhaul of health care. In retrospect his mistake was to set before Congress and the nation a proposal so intricate, with so many moving parts and structural novelties, as to be very hard to explain and difficult to sell in the face of a multimillion dollar negative advertising campaign by private health insurors. Reviewing the recent history of American political reform, from Theodore Roosevelt and Woodrow Wilson on, it is hard to think of a major reform whose salient features could not be explained to the voters in a sentence or two. That was not the case with "managed care" and other intricacies of the Clinton health care reform. In this instance, Bill Clinton the "policy wonk" emerged as the nemesis of Bill Clinton the would-be reformer. If Clinton were to succeed in a second try at a major reform of American health care, that would enter a significant bid for historical attention. So far, however, that and the change in the welfare system (Clinton signed a Republican-sponsored measure that devolved major federal responsibilities on the states and removed the sixty-year-old guarantee of benefits for poor children, and promptly began to campaign against it) have been the only "first rung" issues of his presidency. It remains, so far, a work in progress.

That leaves us with an intriguing question, applicable to all the presidencies examined above: Can presidents consciously arrange their historical reputations? Can they, by taking thought, add cubits to their stature? Presidents who think so can probably find better uses of their time and energy. Apart from the difficulty of guessing what judgments will ultimately be vindicated, which presidents are lucky and which unlucky, "history" is a mercurial thing, far from independent of those who write it. Ages pass and new vistas open; historians change their minds. History proper—the tale that historians tell—is full of gravitational influences that elude direct notice or control but perturb judgment. For more than half a century, the dominant model of presidential performance was, and to an extent still is, Franklin D. Roosevelt's—activist, reformist and often high-handed in dealing with other branches of government. The FDR model, as the historian William Leuchtenburg has observed, cast a long shadow. It not only influenced FDR's successors; it has by influencing our backward glances shaped the ever-shifting evaluation of past presidencies by historians.

When FDR's spell made activism the template of historical significance and success, the reputation of activists like Andrew Jackson and James Knox Polk shot upward. The same standard helped account for the early condescension to Dwight D. Eisenhower, who was, as I noted above, discounted in the 1950s as a "near failure" because he governed deferentially—or appeared to do so.

As later influences have modified the Roosevelt template, Eisenhower's reputation is rising, while the reputations of Jackson and Polk are in steep decline. Vietnam, which came to be viewed as an exercise in deceptive and unchecked presidential activism, highlighted the sneakier aspects of Polk's Mexican War policy, even as moves to redress old wrongs to American Indians have not improved historical regard for Jackson. These changes are typical of the merry-go-round of presidential reputation, although they needn't be taken to mean that historians are shamelessly fickle. The truth is more subtle. Historians respond, as all of us do, to the present and the past—if on the whole more learnedly. They are no less influenced than we are by the passing landmarks, the moods, the shifting sands of an age.

The mercuriality of "history" suggests why presidents are unlikely to enhance their reputations by conscious exertion. Presidents do far better to keep their minds off Clio, the bitchy muse of history. For politicians in office, she is a dangerous heartthrob and, even when won for a day or an hour or a year, a whimsical mistress.

Martin Luther King's Moment

❦

ALTHOUGH DR. MARTIN LUTHER KING's birthday every January is now a national observance, and his a luminous name, he must seem almost as remote to young people, black and white, as a pharaoh of ancient Egypt. Even vivid history evaporates from the popular memory very quickly these days. Without a sense of its historical dimension, however, the revolution that occurred in the standing of Dr. King's people between the end of World War II and his assassination in Memphis in 1968 must be deeply puzzling—as are the conditions that began to be redressed when the Supreme Court first moved against racial discrimination in railway coaches and graduate professional schools in the late 1940s.

Dramatic evidence of this amnesia, at least on the part of whites, emerged when the ex-professional football player O. J. Simpson was acquitted in Los Angeles in 1995 of the murder of his former wife. Surveys suggested that a majority of Simpson's fellow black people approved of the verdict, but also that the black reaction mystified a majority of white people, who believed Simpson transparently guilty. The divided reaction to this celebrity trial seemed to have little to do with the trial evidence but quite a lot to do with a long history which white people are inclined to forget or minimize.

From the landing of the first African slave in America in the early seventeenth century to the framing of the Fourteenth Amendment in 1868, and even for years afterward, law and law enforcement treated black people as second-class citizens. In the Dred Scott decision of 1857, Chief Justice Roger B. Taney sealed the legal caste system by asserting that, at the time of the framing of the Constitution, black people had been considered so far inferior as to enjoy "no rights which a white man is bound to respect." He was doubtless mistaken about the history. Even so, his became the official view of the nation's highest court.

The great southern historian C. Vann Woodward, Sterling Professor of History Emeritus at Yale, has related in his book *The Strange Career of Jim Crow* how a fateful mix of custom, fatigue, accident, racism, cynicism and party wheeling and dealing derailed the Fourteenth Amendment and allowed its central aims to be evaded. In a railroad segregation case of 1896, the Supreme Court ratified discriminatory distinctions in the law, reassuring itself that separation of the races was not in itself discriminatory—that, in effect, the invidious standard announced in the case of *Plessy* v. *Ferguson* lay in the eye of the beholder. Until 1944, the federal courts took the odd view that a political party may select its members by race, as if it were a private club, excluding black people more or less entirely from the electoral process. The juridical fiction that a southern party primary was not a real election stood for decades as the basis of the one-party system, itself the keystone of white supremacy.

In 1948, the young mayor of Minneapolis, Hubert Humphrey (later U. S. senator, vice president and presidential candidate in 1968), urged the Democratic National Convention to make President Truman's civil rights program part of its platform. The issue split the party, provoking a walkout by the delegates from the Deep South. By making subsequent conventions more cautious, moreover, the 1948 experience may actually have delayed the party's embrace of the civil rights cause, although the hesitation was closely bound up with its southern electoral base. Not until 1954 was the "separate but equal" standard of 1896 explicitly reversed by the Supreme Court. As recently as 1963, a dime store in any southern city, though overwhelmingly dependent on the custom of black folk, could require blacks to stand to eat a sandwich at the lunch counter, while white people sat. When the practice was challenged in Greensboro, North Carolina, and other southern cities by youthful black students in the sit-in movement, President Eisenhower described their challenge to the status quo as "disorders."

And then, there was the nearly forgotten fact that the white man's court system had little zeal for intraracial justice. The point was driven home for me one day in the late 1950s when I was a rookie editorialist with the *Charlotte News.* J. E. Dowd, who had edited that fine old afternoon paper when the great W. J. Cash, author of *The Mind of the South,* was writing for it, dropped by my office to comment on a piece I had written about a pending civil rights bill. Dowd was a bright, cordial man with twinkling blue eyes and a raspy voice who chain-smoked with a cigarette holder clinched at a cocky angle, FDR style.

"You know," he said, dribbling ashes on the floor, "the *News* has a long history of crusading for civil rights."

"How so?" I asked politely, concealing my astonishment that this urbane and intelligent man could be so self-deluded. "For one thing," he explained, "we advocated that black on black crime be taken seriously in the courts." Who, I couldn't help asking myself silently, would think of such rudimentary causes as a crusade? Dowd then proceeded to educate me in a little-noticed but pernicious aspect of the Jim Crow system—the casual attitude that prevailed so widely in southern courts regarding what blacks did to one another. There, mayhem on weekend nights was taken for granted, and, however grievous the result, police and judges tended to take a "what else can you expect?" view of it. That legacy of easy condonation may to this day color reactions to the appalling black on black homicide rates in the central cities of America—an epidemic of violence that by the 1980s had made gunshot murder the chief cause of death among young black males under the age of twenty-four and prompted Jesse Jackson to complain that, whereas interracial murder is always a serious crime, "nobody cares" when blacks kill other blacks. Crimes which, if interracial, would command blaring headlines pass all but unnoticed—except, of course, by the families and friends of the victims.

Many southerners of J. E. Dowd's generation, who would have described their views on race as progressive, were pessimistic at the outset about the prospects for the civil rights revolution. The proper groundwork, they argued, had not been laid in patient measures of economic and social improvement—among which they would certainly have listed an elimination of the double standard for black on black crime. Dowd and others who thought as he did were at least half right. They understood before most others that the race issue was in another dimension also a class issue. Every generation is enthralled by its own wisdom and tends to undervalue the wisdom of those who remember the old days. I was a callow young man when Dowd reminded me of his newspaper's earlier "crusade," and I ignorantly scoffed. The failure of perception was not his but mine.

In any case, anyone who was shocked by the reaction of black people to the Simpson verdict (even if the man who beat the charges with the help of a pricy squadron of crafty lawyers was a distinctly odd representative of black consciousness) has slept through American History 101. Perhaps the saddest aspect of this amnesia is that the movement to right the wrongs of segregation, so promisingly begun by Walter White and Roy Wilkins and Thurgood Marshall of the NAACP, and by Dr. King himself, has lately declined into an ideology of victimology. The White-Marshall-King ideal was equality and a chance to be judged as persons, according to the content of one's character and ability. Too often now it has the aspect of a kind of inverted racism.

At least that is the way it often looks, some three decades after Dr. King's death, and the consequence is that blacks and whites routinely fail to understand one another as well as they seemed to do in the heyday of the civil rights revolution. The words of the Kerner Commission of the 1960s—the commission established by

President Johnson and Congress to investigate the causes of the Watts riots in Los Angeles in 1965—are often echoed today: that America is in danger of splitting into two societies, "one black and one white, separate and unequal." There is room for skepticism about that formulation of the problem. The moral questions touching race articulated by Dr. King and others thirty years ago had an almost blinding clarity about them. But today a complex mosaic of legal, social and political relationships lends itself less readily to categorical judgments. Social change seems more problematical, less open to moral suasion.

What is certain is that Dr. King saw more deeply than any other great American since Lincoln into the moral core of the race question. The essence of it as articulated by King and Lincoln is that questions of justice are embedded in the historical situation. Debts accumulate, and their amortization may require us to brace ourselves for a painful and lengthy process. The theme is stated with definitive penetration in Lincoln's Second Inaugural Address:

> If we shall suppose that American slavery is one of those offenses which, in the providence of God, must needs come, but which, having continued through his appointed time, He now wills to remove, and that He gives to both North and South this terrible war, as the woe due to those by whom the offense came, shall we discern therein any departure from those divine attributes which believers in a Living God always ascribe to him? Fondly do we hope—fervently do we pray—that this mighty scourge of war may speedily pass away. Yet, if God wills that it continue, until all the wealth piled by the bondsman's 250 years of unrequited toil shall be sunk, and until every drop of blood drawn with the lash, shall be paid by another drawn with the sword, as was said 3000 years ago . . . "the judgments of the Lord are true and righteous altogether."

Lincoln's biblical eloquence and its continuity with Dr. King's one hundred years later suggest to me that the century separating Lincoln from Dr. King is in certain rhetorical ways shorter than the decades that separate us from Dr. King. He came before us opportunely, at what has proved to be the end of the long era of American popular acquaintance with scriptural language and examples. The critic George Steiner has observed that "the lapse of the

scriptural from the everyday in the commerce of ideas and proposals, of warning and of promise in our body politic in the West,
entails a veritable breakdown of solidarity, of concord within dis-
sent. The fragmentation of discourse is precisely that of Babel."
Even when Dr. King flourished, biblical typology was fading, and
the loss is well advanced in public discourse today. Biblical proto-
types and paradigms—of suffering servants, of blindness and wickedness in the high and mighty and virtue in the lowly, of bondage
under alien taskmasters, of the redemption of enemies through love
and suffering, of the transcendent value of the prophetic voice—
remained intact enough to matter in Dr. King's moment. For whatever the stage of their moral perception, white southerners tended
to be versed in that language and could not ignore it.

I still recall a letter to the editor that came one day to my native
city's *Greensboro Daily News*, for which I was then writing, when the
1964 civil rights bill was pending in the U. S. Senate. The writer
was the venerable Louis R. Wilson, the former university librarian
at Chapel Hill, a cherubic spark of a man. Dr. Wilson wrote: "I
have written to my cousin Sam Ervin in Washington to say that he
is, at this late hour, upholding the hand of the Pharaoh to keep the
children of Israel in bondage." He did not need to explain the powerful imagery of the Exodus. Sam Ervin, then the senior U. S. senator from North Carolina, was a good and just man, but he was
taking the conventional political view of the civil rights bill and
joining in the filibuster by southern senators that ultimately failed
to stop this long-overdue legislation. I suspect that his cousin's letter hit home in his richly furnished soul.

It is astonishing to recall today how modest were the goals of the
revolution Dr. King led. In the Alabama bus boycott of the late
1950s, Dr. King and his followers in the Montgomery Improvement Association did not seek the full racial integration of the
buses, which was shortly to be ordered by the courts. They sought
an arrangement under which blacks would seat themselves on
crowded buses from back to front, first come, first served, and not
be required by custom (as Mrs. Rosa Parks had been ordered but
refused to do) to surrender seats to late-boarding whites. As true
conservatives understand, such are the pebbles that start landslides,

especially when the powerful won't budge on the subject of pebbles. By the time of the bus boycott and the sit-ins that followed it
a year or so later, themselves the first stirrings of direct action and
passive resistance, the segregation of public facilities was a rotten
fabric, ready to fall to tatters at a touch of humanity and common
sense. But even as late as 1960, when the battle over seating at
dime store lunch counters began in Greensboro, that was far from
evident to all, or even to a majority, even indeed to a president of
the United States.

It is well to remember all this rather recent history when we are
tempted to preen ourselves on the American record of justice, and
when we feel an urge to preach on the subject of basic human rights
to those elsewhere who still sit in darkness. It is among our great
American susceptibilities to cherish our myths of exceptionalism
and special virtue. When the history fails to fit the myths, we bend
the history. And the widespread befuddlement by the black reaction
to the Simpson decision suggests that when that last expedient fails,
we simply choose to forget.

CONSTITUTIONAL
DIVINATIONS

The Constitution after Two Centuries

WHEN THE NATION CELEBRATED two centuries of the Constitution in 1987, the American Bar Association, meeting in New Orleans, spotlighted a poll suggesting that "Americans are woefully ill-informed about the content and meaning of the Constitution." Nearly 60 percent of those responding failed to identify the first ten amendments as the Bill of Rights, and 64 percent thought the Constitution established English as the nation's official language. Sixty-one percent thought we needed a new constitutional convention—a strange sentiment if, as the poll suggested, they know so little about the Constitution we have.

Greater constitutional literacy would be preferable. But the poll is otherwise neither more nor less disturbing than a demonstration that 60 percent of Americans fly in modern aircraft without having the foggiest notion of what a fan-jet engine is or how an airfoil functions. There is a puritanical view in some quarters that those who remain ignorant of the mechanics of life do not deserve its benefits. A more charitable operating principle prevails. Desirable in theory, constitutional literacy in practice is not only inessential but unobtainable, because constitutions, like complex machines, are made and maintained by the few for the benefit of the many.

Like most successful plans of government, the Constitution of 1787 was the handiwork of an oligarchy, and most of its durable features may be traced to that fact. It was framed on questionable popular authority—its makers claimed to be revising the old constitution, known as the Articles of Confederation. The fifty-five framers performed radical surgery with a clearer notion of need than mandate from the constituents they represented, who in any case were not a mass electorate. They worked in the name of "the people of the United States," but could afford to deliberate in secret and in indifference to "public opinion" in the modern sense.

The ratification process was similarly "elitist," as we would no doubt say today. A few hundred delegates to state ratifying conventions threshed out the issues without bothering to check polls, which fortunately had not been invented. One of the crucial ratification battlegrounds was Virginia, which had proposed the basic plan for the new constitution. In June 1788 the anti-federalists, as opponents of ratification were called, rang the rafters at the Virginia convention under the leadership of the celebrated orator Patrick Henry. Henry professed to fear "an alarming transition . . . to a consolidated government," as revolutionary as the earlier revolt against the king of England.

By "consolidation," Henry and his allies meant centralization of power. Henry sounded a familiar tocsin, and its echoes have never died out. The final pattern of ratification offers a clue to the basic argument of the anti-federalists. In the small states on the new nation's periphery, from New England to Georgia, strong unionists handily won the battle for ratification. These small fry feared the predatory designs of the superpowers of the day—England, Spain and France—whose territorial claims still bordered American territory north, south and west of the narrow tier of seaboard states.

In the larger, more secure middle states, notably Virginia, Pennsylvania and New York, the antiratification forces were far more articulate and influential. The flavor of their opposition may be sampled in Henry's speeches to the Virginia convention. Henry rather strangely equated liberty with unbridled majoritarianism. Government, he argued, would remain free so long as it was close to the people. Centralization or "consolidation" would distance government from them. Henry noted how hard it would be to amend the new document. If a corporal's guard of opponents could frustrate fundamental change, he asked, what hope could there be for liberty?

Others—for instance, Thomas Wilson, also a Virginian—feared that the new scheme of government would "quickly terminate in absolute monarchy introduced by some bloodthirsty president who will swim to the throne . . . his vessel guided by the soldiers." Such rhetorical worries, which sound grotesquely overwrought now, were more understandable in the late eighteenth century. Republicanism must have seemed to Henry, Wilson and other anti-federalists an all-or-nothing proposition; the conventional political theory of the age held that power was indivisible. A strong central government must necessarily devour smaller rivals, and personal liberty along with them.

These uncritical majoritarian views, so strange to the ears of those of us weaned on James Madison's checks and balances theory, rested on a vision of an idyllic and pastoral God-fearing, homely, decentralized republic—more like a congeries of city-states where neighbor would rule neighbor, under local vines and fig trees. It was an appealing vision. But what might have been the fate of the infant republic if the anti-federalists had prevailed? Would the new nation have dissolved in trade wars, as seemed distinctly likely to Madison and Washington, coming to look a bit like the Germanic empire of that time? We can only guess at the alternative destiny Henry and the anti-federalists had in mind. It was a road not taken.

By gentleman's agreement at several ratifying conventions, it was understood to be a precondition of crucial votes in favor of the new constitution that the missing Bill of Rights would speedily be added, and the first ten amendments were soon supplied by the First Congress. The 1991 bicentennial of the Bill of Rights therefore came swiftly on the heels of the 1987 bicentennial. The celebratory chatter about the Bill of Rights left the rather misleading impression that it had stood virtually alone for two centuries against abuses of personal liberty. I would be the last to underrate the Bill of Rights, but as a matter of history the story is quite different. Except as an intangible ideal and example, the Bill of Rights for the first 166 years of its life had surprisingly little direct effect on the way Americans governed themselves. It allowed nearly as much repression as it prevented.

This is more than contrarian heresy. The Bill of Rights was there in 1798 when Congress, whipped into a state of hysteria by the French Revolution and the European conflicts it spawned, enacted the Alien and Sedition Acts. Politicians were gagged, "aliens" (if unduly critical of the Federalist president and Congress) were deported. Editors were prosecuted and jailed, not for lying but for expressing views deemed disrespectful or seditious. This early epidemic of repression was fortunately brief. The election of Thomas Jefferson in 1800 brought it to an end. His adminstration treated the Sedition Act as a dead letter.

To cite a rather different example, the Bill of Rights was there in 1878 when the Supreme Court, in a puzzling construction of the "free exercise" of religion clause of the First Amendment, held that Mormons could not practice polygamy. Monogamy is the only lawful form of wedlock in America, any religious doctrine to the contrary notwithstanding. And again, the Bill of Rights did not prevent a miscarriage of due process after the Japanese attack on Pearl Harbor in 1941, when many citizens of Japanese ancestry were deprived of liberty and property (see "Skeletons in the National Closet"). Even the writ of habeas corpus did not avail.

Does this dim history mean that the Bill of Rights was unimportant? Like all great charters of personal liberty, it has stood all along as a rebuke to abuses of power, whether the abuse was forced confessions, warrantless wiretapping, or the persecution of political eccentrics in school and college classrooms. The history suggests, however, that the most effective barriers against the abuse of personal liberty are the customs and attitudes inherent in the political culture, which in normal times are reasonably tolerant. When the national mood grows mean and repressive, as it did in the McCarthyist period of the early 1950s, officeholders usually discover ways to curtail civil liberties, and judges find excuses to go along, as they did then.

American liberties, in short, rest on more than mere constitutional impediments to the exercise of power. Madison, principal author of the Bill of Rights, distrusted "parchment barriers," by which he meant written formulae. He thought that structural tensions and rivalries work better than principles, though he considered sound structural principles vitally important. His explanation in The Federalist 51 has not yet been improved upon: "If men were angels, no government would be necessary. If angels were to govern men, neither external nor internal controls on government would be necessary. In framing a government of men over men, the great difficulty lies in this: you must first enable the government to control the governed: and in the next place oblige it to control itself."

The first century and a half of American national experience vindicated Madison's view. Checks and balances worked more effectively than lists of rights as safeguards of liberty. Not until well into the third decade of the twentieth century did the Bill of Rights begin to be fully animated by Supreme Court interpretation and achieve real purchase in daily life. By a process extending over some three decades, the first ten amendments were "absorbed," as the judicial term had it, into the liberty guarantees of the Fourteenth Amendment. The yelps of police-state partisans attested that the Bill of Rights was at last beginning to have real bite in American life.

Even as the constitutional bicentennial observance was in progress, Col. Oliver North of the U. S. Marine Corps appeared before a joint congressional committee inquiring into the so-called Iran/Contra scandal. The escapade, murky in its particulars, touched off a full-dress congressional inquiry. North and others had arranged a secret sale of high-tech weapons from Israeli inventories to allegedly "moderate" factions of the Iranian revolutionary government and the "diversion" of the proceeds from that sale to insurgents who were attempting to overthrow the socialist government of Nicaragua.

The Reagan administration's aggressive policy in Nicaragua had been checked, at least in theory, by congressional restrictions on U. S. aid. It thus appeared that the Reagan administration had executed an end run around those restrictions. North, a saucy and telegenic young officer who later parlayed his notoriety into a radio talk show and the near miss of a U. S. Senate seat in Virginia, was not abashed by his congressional interrogators.

Behind a show of formal deference, the gist of North's response to them was that the president is a one-man band in foreign policy. Congress, North seemed to say, has no business trying to obstruct the discharge of this exclusive responsibility. North's constitutional learning was not extensive, but he made up for the lack in bravado and, such are television impressions, soon became a figure of heroic impudence. In the teledrama of the hearings, North was clearly the winner in popular ratings, whether or not his constitutional views made sense—and usually they didn't.

Had it not been for Sen. George Mitchell of Maine, the Senate majority leader and a former federal judge, on the committee, North would have gotten away with more heresy than he did. Mitchell was present when North held forth on the 1936 Supreme Court decision in *United States* v. *Curtiss-Wright Corporation*. The case involved an embargo power delegated by Congress to President Roosevelt—interim authority to halt U. S. arms shipments to two warring Latin American nations. The Curtiss-Wright company challenged the embargo as an illegitimate delegation of power. Rebuffing the challenge, the Supreme Court cited the words of George Washington: that the president is the nation's "sole organ" in foreign policy. The usual understanding of the dictum is that the nation can speak authoritatively only with one voice in foreign policy. It has never been held to mean, as North suggested, that presidents, let alone their unelected aides, are free to make foreign policy in spite of what Congress thinks.

When Mitchell challenged North's interpretation, the cocky marine colonel dashed for cover, complaining of the one-sidedness of any constitutional joust between a former judge and a mere infantry colonel. His modesty faded when Senator Mitchell was not on hand to contradict him.

It was North's contention that Congress's principal responsibility in foreign policy matters is to stay out of sensitive executive operations, even when their legality is suspect, as certainly was the case with some of North's activities in Ronald Reagan's name. A president need only sign a "finding" (even retroactively) so as to hedge his secret operations with the talismanic label "covert operation," and Congress was obliged to play dead. Such was constitutional law according to North. As a crowning touch, North added that when a president is denied congressional funding, it is perfectly proper (and constitutional) to solicit funds from private donors. But as Justice Robert Jackson wrote in the more pertinent steel seizure case of 1952, when President Truman without congressional authorization directed his commerce secretary to take over a whole industry to avert a strike: "When the President takes measures incompatible with the expressed or implied will of Congress [as had been done in the Iran/Contra affair] his power is at its lowest ebb. . . . For what is at stake is the equilibrium established by our constitutional system."

North's licentious doctrine of presidential power acknowledged no such "equilibrium." His view was not only contrary to the Curtiss-Wright rule (President Roosevelt was exercising a delegated power, and had never pretended otherwise); it ignored the ancient rivalry between the executive and Congress for the "privilege" of setting American foreign policy. Mitchell might well have asked North where in Article II of the Constitution he found the Caesar-like authority he claimed for the president. He might also have reminded the colonel that the power of the purse belongs to Congress and is exclusive. If a president's aides, operating without his knowledge or consent, may legally pass the hat to eccentric millionaires to finance any enterprise they fancy, anywhere in the world, there is no limit on "foreign entanglements" into which we might all be dragged.

In his invocation of a naive legalism, however, Colonel North was thinking very much as a man of his time. The framers of the Constitution had sought, with a craftsman's care, to draw large dynamic effects from limited means. Among those means, none was more vital than the separation of powers: "an essential precaution in favor of liberty," as Madison called it.

This separation cannot be absolute, but until Congress passed the Ethics in Government Act of 1976, one of several misguided reactions to the Watergate scandal, it had stood fairly intact. Section VI of the ethics act introduced a novelty—a procedure for naming special prosecutors to investigate executive scandal who are accountable not to the executive branch but to a special federal court. It is now possible for any important executive branch official to be investigated, tried, sentenced, and the case reviewed—all by the same branch of government.

The history of this noxious experiment begins with the firing of Archibald Cox as Watergate special prosecutor on the evening of October 20, 1973, in a dispute with President Richard M. Nixon over legal control of Nixon's voice-activated White House tape recordings. Special prosecutors up until then had been an unusual but sometimes useful adjunct, in very special instances, to the self-policing capacities of executive government. They had always been independent up to a point, depending on their charters, as Cox was. But they were always presidential appointees, and were understood to be executive officers, deriving their authority from the president and accountable to him. Since its decision in *Myers* v. *U.S.* in 1925, the Supreme Court had taken the view that a president could not meet his constitutional responsibility to "take care that the laws be faithfully executed" if subordinates were independent of his authority.

It was this traditional understanding of the role, powers and functions of special prosecutors—"independent counsel," in the sanitized term now used—that was thought to be discredited by the "firestorm" surrounding Nixon's firing of Cox. In truth, Robert Bork, as acting attorney general, hastened to appoint an effective successor, Leon Jaworski, a former president of the American Bar Association and a man of integrity and intelligence; Jaworski finished the job Cox had begun. Public opinion, offended and alarmed by Nixon's summary firing of Cox (an act that precipitated the resignation of Atty. Gen. Elliot Richardson and his deputy), insisted on having a new special prosecutor. That was surely the central lesson of the affair. It vindicated Madison's notion that countervailing political forces would protect liberty more effectively than "parchment barriers." But the point was missed. The faith of Congress and the public in the capacity of presidents and their departments of justice to police themselves had been fatally impaired, and, in the age of media politics, what mattered was not the reality—Jaworski's effective completion of Cox's mission—but the appearances.

Following the Cox uproar, no fewer than eight different bills proposing various forms of independence for special prosecutors were introduced. In the ultimate flight of whiggery, even the sensible Sen. Sam J. Ervin, Jr., of North Carolina, an early hero of the Watergate investigation, went so far as to propose the amputation of the Department of Justice from all presidential control. At least that erosion of presidential accountability was rejected, though the conduct of Atty. Gen. Janet Reno during the Clinton presidency suggested a de facto independence.

A common denominator of almost all the proposals for legislative action was that special prosecutors would be independently appointed and accountable to someone other than the president—a panel of federal judges, as it turned out. Their appointment could be precipitated by the barest rumor of scandal unless the attorney general could certify that the charges were frivolous. In 1988, in the case of *Morrison* v. *Olson*, the Supreme Court by a surprising vote of seven to one turned aside a challenge to the law's constitutionality.

As Terry Eastland, a former press chief at the Department of Justice, observes in his acute book *Ethics, Politics and the Independent Counsel* (1990), the independent counsel law marks a historic departure. The framers' solution to occasional misconduct in high office was structural and political, not legalistic. They assumed, correctly as the Watergate affair itself proved, that abuses of power would arouse balancing and checking forces, including, in cases of grave misconduct, the ultimate sanction of impeachment and ejection. There is no evidence that they were mistaken. But after half a century of uncritical faith in strong executive government, Vietnam and Watergate brought on a mood of disillusionment. Once uncritically revered, the presidency was redesignated as "imperial"; legalistic devices for the restraint of Caesarism became fashionable, no matter what deformity they might bring to the framers' design.

Today, American government is everywhere beset by a tendency to substitute "prolix legal codes" (Chief Justice John Marshall's dismissive term in *McCulloch* v. *Maryland* for legalism parading as constitutionalism) for institutional and political dynamics. The elegant functionalism of the framers' plan is now in danger of being smothered by legalism. This is in part no doubt the result of a surplus of lawyers who know more of tort and contract than of the Federalist papers or Madisonian constitutional theory. It is the kind of constitutional error we normally expect the Supreme Court to correct. But a court that had gagged on the delegation of relatively minor ministerial powers of budget sequestration by the Gramm-Rudman budget act swallowed without blinking the assignment of vast inquisitorial and prosecutorial powers to creatures of the courts. In so doing, it made nonsense of the clause of Article III that provides for the appointment of "such inferior officers" as Congress may think fit by other than the president—a provision plainly intended to allow judges to appoint clerks of court, or Congress its own staff. The incidental effects of the special prosecutor law include a tendency to trivialize great issues by "criminalizing" policy disputes—by turning them into exercises in legalism. A ridiculous low point was reached when officials of the Clinton administration explained, in 1996, that they would undertake no internal investigation of the mysterious appearance of FBI personnel files at the White House personnel security office because any paper trail they might create would speedily be subpoenaed by Congress and/or a special prosecutor and the internal investigative procedure itself made an issue.

The Constitution as it came from the hands of the framers more than two centuries ago provides ample structural protection against abuses of power and trust. That has been proved time and again. What it does not do is to give the policing of ethical misconduct precedence over the vital requirement of energetic government and an accountable presidency. That is the constitutional heresy that came with the "independent counsel" statute in 1976, and the end is not yet in sight.

A Good Word for the Framers

୶

As AMERICAN POLITICAL PRACTICE evolves, the national thraldom to what Henry Adams called "the democratic dogma" seems to deepen—so much so that it often clouds our appreciation of the uses of political complexity.

The framers of the Constitution were very much of the opposite view. They clearly wished to distance government from mob spirit and made institutional arrangements to that end. Thus we don't really vote directly for presidents but for electors whose names we seldom know; originally those electors, who usually were known, had discretion to vote for whomever they chose. Thus five Supreme Court justices, appointed for life during "good behavior," may nullify the wishes of 535 elected members of Congress by declaring a popular law unconstitutional. And while the unlimited debate rule in the Senate is customary rather than constitutional, a long-winded senator or two may thwart the will of a huge majority. Delay, dilution, obstruction. The framers were untroubled by dilatory devices, for they feared intemperate and impulsive acts far more.

Today, these survivals of an earlier view of republicanism are usually damned out of hand as inconsistent with democratic theory, as if that complaint alone sets them beyond the pale of decency. But there is little evidence that the populist fashions of the present are superior to the old devices—and some evidence that they actually defeat democratic consensus. In the name of democracy, for instance, we now delegate vital decisions (notably in the nomination of presidential candidates) to small, self-selected and unrepresentative "single-issue" groups whose only qualification is their own willfulness. That is the essence of the process by which would-be presidents are chosen today, usually well before the national conventions meet to ratify the choice. Nearly every state now conducts a presidential primary, the earlier the better, and primaries in their own way can be utterly unrepresentative. Even more unrepresentative are the devices of initative and referendum adopted by several western states during the Progressive Era. In theory they bring government and lawmaking closer to "the people." In practice, they often exclude large numbers from the lawmaking process. In California, for instance, whose referendum measures are often revolutionary, and whose politics are utterly dominated by television—thus extraordinarily susceptible to the influence of money—scores of "propositions" (potential laws and constitutional amendments), many of them complicated or obscure, appear on the ballot by petition. Vast sums of money are spent explaining, promoting or opposing them, and voters often need catalog-length glosses just to know what they're voting on. As an alternative to representative government—which is what the framers of the U. S. Constitution meant by "republican" government—direct democracy has glaring. flaws. But those flaws infrequently prompt us to call it into question.

All this would seem to constitute a good argument for a revival of historical, rather than ideological, thinking about how American political institutions were intended to function—and perhaps even a revival of sympathy for the usefulness of informed delegation.

But it is hard to get a hearing for heresy when those most responsible for preserving the spirit of the framers attack or patronize them. In the spring of 1987, as the nation was in the midst of celebrating two centuries under the Constitution, the late Justice Thurgood Marshall was seized by an impish urge to rain on the bicentennial parade. He did so in a speech to the American Bar Association in Hawaii, the burden of which was that the Constitution was "defective from the start" and had needed many repairs to sustain "the individual freedoms and human rights we hold as fundamental today."

There is obviously something to be said for that view. The only tenable defense of some original features of the document—a twenty-year reprieve for the slave trade, for instance—is the one the framers themselves pled: without that and other compromises that look a bit sordid now, the South probably would not have joined the new union. In consequence, a loose and disintegrating confederation would then have remained in peril of complete collapse. That is the irony. Had the confederation as it was collapsed, and the slave states gone their own way, Abraham Lincoln would have lacked the weapon of unionist sentiment that served him so well in 1861.

But even the "defective" Constitution of 1787 took an indispensable step toward a better world for those the framers left behind or out. Under the Articles of Confederation, which were amendable only by unanimous consent of all the states and which entirely lacked a federal judiciary to enforce any national law, slavery would have been infinitely more secure than the new Constitution left it. Without a federal court system, the civil rights revolution of the 1950s and 1960s would hardly have been conceivable.

Marshall told his audience that "while the Union survived the Civil War, the Constitution did not. In its place arose a new, more promising basis for justice and equality, the Fourteenth Amendment, ensuring protection of the life, liberty and property of all persons." True, in fact. This is the essence of the "living Constitution" doctrine to which Justice Marshall adhered during his three decades on the bench. It is an essential axiom of the judicial activism he practiced. But since Marshall had argued the school segregation cases as chief counsel for the NAACP, he had every reason to recall that the Fourteenth Amendment had been an unreliable weapon in the battle for racial equality. Even a sympathetic Supreme Court, after two rounds of briefing and argument in the school cases, failed to discover a clear mandate against school segregation in the Fourteenth Amendment. Where, then, did it discover the constitutional values that gave Marshall and his clients victory in 1954 against "separate but equal" school systems that were flagrantly unequal? In that "defective" original document.

Which is to say that the argument over the implications of the Constitution for black citizenship and equality did not begin in 1868, with the framing of the Fourteenth Amendment. It began well before that. Otherwise, Lincoln would have lacked a leg to stand on in his attack on the Supreme Court's ruling in the Dred Scott case of 1857, whose holding was that black people were not citizens and had "no rights which a white man is bound to respect." Thurgood Marshall found a seam in our seamless constitutional fabric that is largely imaginary. The Fourteenth Amendment was not a graft but a branch of the old trunk and draws its vitality from it.

Among the perennial complaints of the original design that Thurgood Marshall found "defective," none is more persistent than complaints about the presidential electoral system. Any third-party candidacy is sure to bring the worriers out of the woodwork, as did the "reform" candidacy of Texas billionaire Ross Perot in 1992. Even people of substantial political wisdom and discernment, including Lloyd Cutler (sometime White House counsel to both Carter and Clinton) and Norman Ornstein (the American Enterprise Institute's resident guru on matters congressional) were shuddering over hypothetical scenarios. The danger, they thought, was that a deadlocked electoral vote might throw the choice of the next president into the House of Representatives. And what if the House, crowded with new members, failed to choose? What if the vice president, separately chosen by the Senate, became "acting president"?

None of these hypothetical horrors materialized, which is part of the point. Few ever do. But in a way, the hysteria aside, these anxieties serve a useful purpose. Every now and then it is well to remind ourselves that the American form of government isn't simple and wasn't intended to be, on grounds articulated by the great English Whig, Edmund Burke: "The simple forms of government are fundamentally defective to say no more of them." Such fetishes as "efficiency" and "democracy" (of the "one man, one vote" variety, anyway) have great emotional appeal. But neither, after all, is or was intended to be a paramount constitutional value. James Madison and the other framers preferred procedural complexity and inefficiency. Their objective was to avoid rash policymaking by making decisions difficult—not to grease the wheels of government so that they would turn as fast as possible.

In fact, apropos of the anxieties of 1992, the country has never actually been the worse for those occasional elections (1800, 1824, 1876) when the unusual happened and an indecisive or contested electoral vote gave the backup machinery a workout. There is a dogmatic view today that mass voting is the best way to choose presidents, but it is a relatively late view. According to Max Farrand, editor of the classic edition of Madison's Notes on the 1787 constitutional convention, there is considerable evidence that the framers expected the electoral college to function most of the time as a nominating mechanism and the House of Representatives, in the usual case, actually to elect the president. And more to the point, can it be seriously argued that mass democracy has produced a better run of presidents than Washington, Adams, Jefferson, Madison, Monroe and John Quincy Adams?

I occasionally try to imagine what would happen, in the present climate, if the work of 1787 had to be done all over again. How would it go?

Begin with the fact that the fifty-five participants, including the dozen or so who really mattered, devoted a whole summer to the drafting of the document—more than a summer, if you count James Madison's diligent preparation. Obviously, for all their reluctance to invest the time, none seems to have felt the investment was wasted. All had other anxieties. Washington's letters to his farm manager at Mount Vernon show that he fretted about his carrot beds and fruit trees. There are persons of constitution-making caliber among us (my list would include Lloyd Cutler, Griffin Bell, Lewis Powell, Daniel Patrick Moynihan, Dan Boorstin and others), but could they afford the time? And even if we assembled a current version of that "gathering of demigods" (as Jefferson called it), competing distractions would require, as all such enterprises seem to do nowadays, a staff of hundreds. The original convention made do with a staff of one, its secretary, Maj. William Jackson.

Another threat would arise from the endless importunings of single-minded fanatics and zealots, ranging from ethnic and feminist lobbies to military/industrial spoilsmen, all spending millions of dollars on advertising to keep their case in the public eye. On their heels would come the press and the electronic media, with whirring cameras and glaring lights and petitions for court injunctions against closed meetings. The *New York Times* would fulminate against "secret convenants, secretly arrived at." If a task force designated by President Clinton to plan a new health insurance proposal for the nation under the chairmanship of Hillary Rodham Clinton was forced in 1993 into public deliberations that helped the insurance lobby destroy the plan before it took flight, imagine what would be said of a convention writing a new constitution.

But even if the convention managed to keep its doors closed, an armada of investigative reporters would fill the air and the newspapers with lurid leaks and speculations. For reasons no historian has ever pinned down, dire rumors circulated at one point during the summer of 1787 that the bishop of Osnaburgh, a younger son of George III, would be named first king of the United States. A newspaper published a list of delegates rumored to be willing to establish a monarchy, and a disclaimer had to be issued. Multiply the Osnaburgh caper a thousandfold and amplify it with the instant reach of cable television news, and try to picture success. Perhaps the killer would be a garbled account of Alexander Hamilton's speech of June 18, in which, among other elitist ideas, he called for senators chosen for life and state governors appointed by Congress. In Philadelphia, word of this never got out. Today, there would be leaks and rioting in the streets.

But even if all these barriers were successfully hurtled, surely the convention could not, today, withstand the massed fury of outraged public piety. Among the fifty-five at Philadelphia, there was not so much as a single holy man or spiritual guru, not one. When it was leaked, as it surely would be, that Dr. Benjamin Franklin's proposal for daily prayer had been dismissed as a pointless extravagance, there would be hell to pay. Or heaven. And supposing that this impious gathering of rationalists and deists had written a Constitution omitting all reference to God Almighty, save by implication in the pointed exclusion of religious tests for office? Sodom and Gomorrah again, only worse. The hosts of righteousness would march on Independence Hall and the delegates would flee through a rear door, lucky not to be felled by a bolt of lightning sent in divine displeasure.

In short, a repeat of the "miracle at Philadelphia" is all but inconceivable, and that ought to make us a bit more careful about underestimating the miraculous nature of the original document left to us.

The Mysteries of "Original Intent"

WHEN EDWIN MEESE III, Ronald Reagan's friend and sometime attorney general, summoned the nation's judges to "a jurisprudence of original intent" one day in 1986, he detonated a controversy that echoed along the Potomac for the better part of a decade.

The echoes rang a bit hollow, however, insofar as they implied that the "original intent" of the framers of the Constitution is historically self-evident or easily pried from dusty documents. The distinguished constitutional scholar Leonard Levy, who holds strong views in such matters and rarely understates them, retorted that any originalist theory of constitutional construction is a "will-o'-the-wisp." Levy takes pleasure in showing that not even the mythic heroes of the American legal past have honored any such theory of constitutional construction, even in those instances when it might be ascertained. He suggests, for instance, that the most revered jurist in our history, Chief Justice John Marshall, was among the worst offenders against "original intent," deliberately violating the framers' purposes on several critical occasions.

One such instance was Marshall's ruling in *Marbury v. Madison*, the 1803 landmark decision in which the Supreme Court first asserted its power to review the constitutionality of acts of Congress. In so doing, the Court invalidated parts of the Judiciary Act of 1789. But, as Levy points out, that act had been primarily the work of two actual framers, Oliver Ellsworth and William Patterson. Did Marshall, who had not been present in Philadelphia in 1787, know better than Ellsworth and Patterson, who had been, what powers of original jurisdiction they had "originally intended" to bestow upon the Supreme Court? Marshall risked that presumption, and it enabled him to assert a major power (judicial review of acts of Congress) by denying his court a trivial one (the issuance of writs of mandamus in cases of original jurisdiction). Insofar as judicial review rests on the reasoning of *Marbury* v. *Madison*, Levy asserts, "it rests on rubbish"—again, Levy is not given to understatement.

But what, if anything, could Edwin Meese and Judge Robert Bork (Reagan's failed nominee to the Court, whose confirmation hearings in the late summer of 1987 were an epic airing of such issues) mean by "original intent"? Some years ago, when the topic was hot, I essayed an answer in a talk in Williamsburg, at a seminar on constitutional interpretation sponsored by the Institute of Early American History and Culture, of which I was then a trustee. I ventured to describe the search for original intent as a process of "divination" (the very word used by Justice Robert Jackson and others to describe its difficulty in certain areas of constitutional construction) and, as years pass, the word still seems right. I offered by way of illustration the curiosities and difficulties underlying a case then pending—this was 1988—before the U. S. Supreme Court.

Late in its 1987 term, the Court surprised almost everyone, including the parties to an otherwise routine racial discrimination case, by voting to revisit a decade-old decision, *Runyon* v. *McCrary*. The Court in that case had held that a *private* act of racial discrimination—namely, denying admission to a private school on the basis of race—was barred by the 1866 Civil Rights Act. For nearly a century, until the Warren Court began to rule otherwise in various cases, the courts had assumed the contrary. Certainly Congress had so assumed, when it passed the public accommodations title of the

1964 Civil Rights Act. If the new interpretation of the old act was right, Congress had wasted much time and breath on the debate over whether discrimination at that mythic institution "Mrs. Murphy's boarding house" (a hypothetical small private business) could be barred under the Commerce Clause.

The Court's sudden revisitation of *Runyon v. McCrary* raised, in its purest state, an issue of "original intent." Congress had passed the 1866 Civil Rights Act between the Thirteenth Amendment, outlawing slavery, and the Fourteenth Amendment, which is usually thought of as a second, or supplementary, constitution, embodying the contemporary sense of what the Civil War had decided. Under its Thirteenth Amendment enforcement powers, Congress had tried to counter the "black codes" that were springing up around the postbellum South—state and local ordinances that sought to substitute peonage and other forms of physical control of freedmen for slavery itself. The 1866 act guaranteed to all U. S. citizens "the same right in every state and territory to make and enforce contracts, to sue, be parties, given evidence, and to the full and equal benefit of all laws and proceedings for the security of persons and property as is enjoyed by white citizens."

Clearly, no state or official could impair those rights; that would be a federal offense. The question was whether Congress also meant to bar certain forms of private discrimination as well. We all make minor choices that are so personal, or so trivial (for instance the hiring of a baby sitter for one's children, or someone to clean house or mow the lawn) that we are free to "discriminate" as arbitrarily as we please. The rule of *de minimis* ("the law takes no account of trifles") applies. But there may be contractual engagements of a more consequential kind in which private discretion could arguably be limited by law in the public interest. If so, what might they be? The 1866 act, which long was agreed to enjoy a quasi-canonical authority regarding the meaning of the Fourteenth Amendment, never answered that question clearly. It gradually fell into disuse, and the wording of the Fourteenth Amendment suggested in any case that the thrust of these early concerns with civil rights was to protect blacks against "state action," not private prejudice. That became the consensus of judicial opinion as to "original intent" until the Warren Court changed it. Apparently, the legislative history of the 1866 act throws ambiguous light, at best, on the issue; the text itself is no more illuminating. Meanwhile, the expansive reading of the act in the Runyon decision in 1976 had become a fount of damage claims against private individuals.

In this revisitation of the Runyon precedent, we had a clearly defined "original intent" inquiry involving a twilight zone of policy, where legislative and judicial powers overlap. Constitutional purists invariably speak and write as if these two powers may be, and should be, surgically separated. But the history of the 1866 civil rights act shows the difficulty. Congress has often found it convenient to allow judges to elaborate legislative policy, even if the elaboration changes meaning as judges change, or as judges change their minds. That may not fit the nicer notions of the separation of powers, or the more exalted expectations of original intent. But it has been the practice for a long time.

Interestingly, in an amicus curiae brief in the Runyon case, no fewer than 66 U. S. senators and 118 members of the House of Representatives pleaded with the Court to let the later Warren Court interpretation of the 1866 civil rights act stand, barring acts of private discrimination. Among other arguments, they said that silence implies consent: "The Congress has been fully cognizant of how Section 1981 has been construed . . . [and] has rebuffed legislative efforts to reverse that construction. Congressional intent could hardly have been more clear if Congress had reenacted Section 1981 following [the Runyon decision]." Ultimately, the Supreme Court complied with congressional sentiment. It sustained the new view of the 1866 act. History and circumstance can be a problem for those with a naive or simplistic view of "original intent"—who believe, in effect, that it is usually a matter of discovering or recovering the self-evident. It is rarely so, as this instance and many others prove.

The original constitutional materials—including the records of what happened at the 1787 constitutional convention and at the state conventions that ratified the new basic charter—range from fragmentary to nonexistent. James Madison's notes, much the best source, are partial and sometimes cryptic, and Madison himself later derided their importance. And there is more. When the House of Representatives staged its first important debate on the meaning of the new Constitution, eight framers were present as members and participants, and they differed strenuously among themselves. They differed, for instance, as to the intended scope of the president's power to remove his own appointees, an issue that would be long debated. The first Congress debated the charter of the first Bank of the United States, with President Washington and Secretary of the Treasury Alexander Hamilton (for) and Madison (against) differing. All had been present at Philadelphia—Washington and Madison throughout and Hamilton occasionally. On the occasion of that debate, Madison observed that the "Constitution . . . [originally] was nothing more than a dead letter," and that it was the state ratification conventions that gave it "life and vitality . . . by the voice of the people." All very well, but the records of ratification—what the delegates said and what life they thought they were breathing into the new Constitution—are sparser in some states than those of the debate in Philadelphia.

Leonard Levy, again, in books like *Original Intent and the Framers' Constitution* (1988), is illuminating on these historical issues of originalism. But Levy reserves special scorn for the jurists of today, including some for whom Edwin Meese has the highest regard. He censures Chief Justice William Rehnquist for asserting that the First Amendment's Establishment Clause ("Congress shall make no law respecting an establishment of religion") means no more than that the United States may not establish a national church. There is persuasive evidence to the contrary, for the term "an establishment of religion" had a much broader meaning when the Bill of Rights was written. According to Levy, it "meant government aid and sponsorship of religion, principally by impartial tax support of the institutions of religion, the churches." Levy argues that the Establishment Clause was intended to place issues of religious conscience entirely beyond the legislative powers of Congress. With his usual confidence, Levy proclaims that the "non-preferentialists," his term for those who advocate the support of religion with public funds, are dead wrong. In an erudite survey of state "establishments of religion" of the 1780s and after—the period when the First Amendment was born—Levy identifies at least six as plural: systems that authorized taxes to aid one or more sect or church. Such an establishment for the Commonwealth of Virginia would have been effected by Patrick Henry's "assessment bill" of 1784, a measure defeated after long struggle and intrigue by Jefferson and Madison. That struggle was of definitive historical importance because what Madison wrote about the issue in his "Memorial and Remonstrance" (one of the three or four key documents on religious freedom in early America) sheds great light on the attitudes of the key author of the First Amendment.

On this and related historical points, Levy deploys massive evidence. When the framers spoke of "an establishment of religion," they had in mind systems of pluralistic subsidy—not simply of a single church, Anglican or otherwise. They worded the Establishment Clause to warn Congress away from meddling in such matters, pro or con.

Even so, certain questions linger. In its most literal form, Levy's interpretation of the Establishment Clause would force us into a paradoxical and improbable conclusion—that judges, as our appointed constitutional interpreters, may (and do) make judgments as to what is and isn't permissible in church-state relations, while legislators are intended to leave the matter entirely alone. And when Leonard Levy turns from constitutional history to issues of current policy, he is as much of two minds as the rest of us. He denounces the Supreme Court's decision in *Aguilar* v. *Felton*, which threw out New York's use of Title I remedial education funds in parochial schools, as "disastrous," and more than once he seems to argue that courts should wink at "trivial" breaches of the eternal wall between church and state. He is annoyed that the Court would allow Pawtucket, Rhode Island, to exhibit a Christmas crèche on public property, but he seems to suggest that the Court merely gagged on a gnat when it denied Kentucky the right to post the Ten Commandments on classroom bulletin boards, or Alabama permission to allow a moment of silence for optional prayer. In his discussion of Supreme Court interpretations of the Establishment Clause, Levy writes that "the preponderance of evidence suggests that the framers of the 14th Amendment neither intended its provisions to incorporate any part of the Bill of Rights nor to impose on the states limitations imposed on the U. S. only."

That may be so, but if taken literally this view would align Levy with those who claim that by checking state discretion in church-state matters, the federal courts have usurped reserve powers. But we aren't, it seems, to take this historical view seriously, for Levy scorns those who use exactly that argument to deny the legitimacy of Supreme Court restraints on school prayer and other infringements of the First Amendment. If historical intention is basic, then Levy's major premise—that "non-preferential" support for religion is unconstitutional—cannot be good constitutional interpretation for it overlooks the view that "incorporation" is illegitimate. Is some historical evidence stronger than other historical evidence? Or simply less convenient?

In issues of original intent, it must be admitted that Leonard Levy is at least impartial. He is as critical of the liberal justices William Brennan and Thurgood Marshall as of their conservative brethren. Both had said, as justices, that when given the opportunity they would vote to declare the death penalty "cruel and unusual punishment," hence unconstitutional under the Eighth Amendment. Yet as Levy notes, there is no textual or historical warrant for the position and much that refutes it.

By the time Levy has finished with Edwin Meese and various judges, he has made a powerful case that neither now, nor in the past, has anyone paid real deference to "original intent," even when it could be known or guessed with fair confidence. He regards Meese's endorsement of originalism as political sloganeering, an attempt to veil judicial activism (directed to "conservative" policy goals) in the ultimate cloak of respectability. But even if you grant that history's testimony regarding intent is sketchy, and the materials for "a jurisprudence of original intent" scanty, the issue won't quite go away. It is more than a contest over a slogan; it is an argument over the obligation of judges, vested as they are with great power, to move within the limits of some basic rules. But whose rules? The rich constitutionalism of the United States is informed by but not limited to history, and if, as Levy says, the Supreme Court has "flunked history," the burden on those who sit on the bench to rule in the spirit of the Constitution is no lighter for all that.

The amusing and mildly cynical term "law office history" sprang from a well-known lawyerly tendency to rearrange historical evidence to fit a brief. When past intent is at issue, the advocate who marshals the more believable history often wins. As a rule, then, law office history is less reflective than polemical. In perhaps the most famous, and crucial, argument of this sort in modern times, the Supreme Court in 1952 asked parties to the epic cases known collectively as *Brown* v. *Board of Education of Topeka* (the school segregation cases) to brief the specific question of whether or not the framers of the Fourteenth Amendment intended to ban school segregation. The briefs were indecisive, as the Court acknowledged. But it was not because the parties had not bent every resource of research and wit to prove otherwise.

Perhaps, then, even the most inventive quests for "original intent" are law office history, albeit of a superior sort. Certainly originalism (or interpretivism, as the mode of constitutional construction advocated by Edwin Meese and other conservatives came to be called) has itself become a battleground. When the text of a constitutional provision is less than self-interpreting (as many are), and when its origins are cloudy, whose understanding carries authority? And even when original intent may confidently be established, does it mandate a static constitution, from which any deviation except by formal amendment is a betrayal? There are purists—Raoul Berger of the Harvard Law School is one—who insist that that is exactly the case. The Constitution must change by amendment or not at all. And that, by the lights of Leonard Levy and other historians, would make American constitutional history little more than a chronicle of usurpation by judges and politicians. So perhaps the argument proves too much. When the Court and the country are seriously out of phase on vital public issues, as they were for a time in the mid-1930s, and when those differences are felt to be of paramount importance, there must be room for a bit of "play" in the institutional joints. My own modest reading of the relevant history suggests that the framers did not seek rigidity, on the one hand, nor a politicized bench of judges, on the other; nor did they wish for courts that would never, ever, bend with the winds of change. In other words, they wanted exactly the ambiguity, and argument, we seem to have whenever "original intent" becomes an issue.

NATIONALISM AT THE
END OF AN ERA

Historians and the
Enola Gay *Exhibit*

∾

No RECENT PUBLIC CONTROVERSY generated more heat than the disputed planning for the exhibition of the *Enola Gay* in the summer of 1995. The Air and Space Museum's display of the fuselage of the B-29 bomber that dropped the first atomic bomb on Hiroshima was to mark the fiftieth anniversary of the end of the war with Japan.

Many interesting historical questions about the first use of the atomic weapon were quickly submerged by political, martial, nationalistic and moralistic debate—mainly the latter. The discussion became an occasion for the ventilation of prejudices—ready-made views applied to new issues. Few belligerents in this historiographical warfare approached the anniversary in an inquiring frame of mind—neither the American Legion and its allies among the veterans and military organizations nor the historian Gar Alperovitz and his followers, whose argument is that the bomb was used unnecessarily and as a kind of overture to the cold war with the Soviet Union.

A Canadian responding to one of my newspaper columns about the controversy disputed my characterization of the role of revisionism in distorting Harry Truman's purposes in using the Hiroshima bomb. He quoted James F. Byrnes, who, at the time of Hiroshima, had recently become Truman's secretary of state, on the usefulness of using American atomic prowess to render the Russians more pliant in the negotiations on the future of Europe in which Byrnes himself happened to be primarily engaged. Then, characterizing Byrnes as Truman's most influential adviser, he took Byrnes's views as proof that Truman had dropped the atomic bombs for reasons agreeable to Byrnes.

This was a non sequitur and perhaps an irrelevance. Even if Byrnes had been as dominant among Truman's inner circle of counselors as my correspondent claimed, and even if his views on the use of the bomb were noticed and weighed by Truman, it is vastly improbable that they made as much difference as those of Secretary of War Henry L. Stimson and Gen. George C. Marshall, who had been intimate players in high strategy throughout the war and assuredly made the key recommendations concerning the bomb. Byrnes's rank and views in themselves prove nothing. As even Gar Alperovitz has shown, one can assemble a gilt-edged roll of eminent American figures who said all sorts of unfavorable things about the bomb. But citing them also proves nothing about Truman's motives, which he repeatedly explained for himself. In the absence of evidence that he dissembled, historians are obliged to prefer the president's own account of his actions. The random citation of noted figures with strong views, though often cited as historical evidence through the *Enola Gay* controversy, is nothing of the sort unless clear connections can be established between the views expressed and the actions taken.

For this and other reasons, the argument over the *Enola Gay* exhibit was more enlightening as a study in political and moral fervor than in the reasons why President Truman and his advisers thought it necessary to attack Hiroshima and Nagasaki with atomic bombs in August 1945. The first and so far the only use of atomic weapons may have been a calamity for mankind, as it certainly was for the innocent civilians who died in those cities. But in the harsh climate of modern technological warfare, moral judgments require the consideration of alternatives.

Suppose, for instance, that the atomic bombs had not been used in 1945, when fewer than half a dozen existed and all were in American hands, but remained a tempting potentiality of untested destructive power through the worst years of the cold war, when they came to exist in tens of thousands on both sides of the Iron Curtain. Might their use have become more tempting without Hiroshima as a warning? Or, more plausibly, might the nuclear danger have been less a deterrent to violence than it was? Might a Berlin or Cuban crisis have pushed either the United States or the Soviet Union over the brink? I have repeatedly asked this question of several of those who moralize about Hiroshima, but have received no persuasive answer. Some to whom I have addressed the question seem not to grasp its pertinence. Yet such what-ifs illuminate, if they do not resolve, the moral issues historians address. What were the alternatives? That question must always be asked, and answered, as a preliminary to moral judgments about the past.

Younger historians are deeply infected, these days, by fashions that occasionally sound silly or sinister, and the after-the-fact argument about the use of the first atomic weapons proved well suited to engage them. The "new history," as some practitioners call it, is steeped in the conviction that Western culture is "imperialist" and "patriarchal," glorying in masculine and martial values, and that this orientation predisposes it to cruelty and violence against lesser breeds. The *Enola Gay* exhibit, as originally conceived, was colored by these fashionable preoccupations.

World War II, on which Hiroshima rang down the final curtain, has been called the "last good war." But the history even of good wars is a battle over perspective. The dullest student of history has heard that the winners usually write it, although some Japanese—some, I emphasize—have done a good job of obscuring the memory of Pearl Harbor in the memory of Hiroshima. But aside from familiar revisionist motifs, Hiroshima should be an ideal candidate for consensus history. We know a great deal about the setting in which the bomb was used, and why it was used, and the well-attested facts bear slight resemblance to the caricature now gaining ground among revisionists.

The atomic bomb in no sense originated with the intent of enforcing the hegemonic mastery of a Western white race over an Asian people. The atomic bomb was conceived for a single overriding reason: it was feared that Adolf Hitler's scientists would build it first, as they certainly attempted to do. That was the danger that Niels Bohr and Albert Einstein pressed upon President Roosevelt in a famous letter written soon after the war broke out and delivered by their friend and protégé Leo Szilard. Their counsel prevailed. That the German surrender came earlier than the Japanese surrender, in May 1945, and that the bomb was instead used to shorten the Pacific war, was an accident of fate. Had the Normandy invasion failed in June of 1944, more than a year earlier, one can imagine a quite different sequence. In his recent book *"Monty,"* about the British commander in the Allied invasion of Europe, Alistair Horne, the distinguished English military historian, speculates authoritatively that failure at Normandy would have brought "almost certainly . . . the employment of the first atomic bombs in the summer of 1945 on Germany, not Japan."

President Truman and his advisers, in close consultation with the British government, acted in the belief that the Hiroshima bomb would both shorten the war and spare scores of thousands of lives on both sides. The menacing precedent was the invasion of Okinawa, which had been fanatically defended by the Japanese (who believed surrender itself to be dishonorable). Okinawa was regarded as a bloody curtain-raiser for the invasion of the Japanese home islands and a preview of its costs. A million Allied casualties were anticipated in some planning papers for Operation Olympic, the assault on Kyushu, planned for November 1945. The statesmen of 1945 were less conscious than we are now of a difference in kind between nuclear weapons and the conventional high explosives and incendiaries that had already been used with scorching effect against Tokyo, Berlin, Hamburg, and Dresden. Blast and firestorm killed far more civilians in those cities than the atomic weapons would kill, and with a wanton high-tech cruelty that is difficult to differentiate morally from atomic blast and radiation. The devastat-

ing side effects of atomic weapons were still obscure. Lethal radiation sickness had been observed in the laboratories at Los Alamos,
but the controversy over radiactive fallout and Strontium-90 lay
almost a decade in the future.

If these are not facts, there are no agreed-upon historical facts.
The twisting they underwent in the argument over the *Enola Gay*
exhibit is exasperating. But the argument had considerable value as
a clinic in what history is and isn't. It isn't the amassing of facts.
That is usually easy enough. It is an argument over what the facts
prove, once assembled, when they are facts and when they prove
anything, and it is unending. The historian John Lukacs has observed that "history is revisionism . . . the ceaseless reviewing and
revising and rethinking of the past. . . . The historian deals in multi-
ple jeopardy that the law eschews . . . retrying and retrying again."
Learning that lesson may be as important as learning the truth
about the *Enola Gay* and the first use of atomic weapons.

The most prominent and voluble spokesman for the revisionists in
the *Enola Gay* debate was the University of Maryland historian Gar
Alperovitz, the author of *Atomic Diplomacy,* who occasionally offered his good offices in the unlikely role of referee between the
two sides. In fact, however, Alperovitz continues to push the same
views about Hiroshima which he first advanced in his influential
earlier book, in my view one of the most misguided treatises on
American foreign policy since Sen. Joseph McCarthy's ghostwrit-
ten, pseudoscholarly attack on General Marshall. Alperovitz has
softened and qualified his argument since *Atomic Diplomacy* got a
scholarly roasting. But even as revised, there is no "substantial
scholarly acceptance," as he claimed in a *Washington Post* article, of
the argument that the atomic bomb was used with "the hope of
strengthening the West's hand against the Soviet Union." This is a
milquetoast version of his stronger thesis that Truman deliberately
rebuffed Japanese surrender overtures so as to drop the bomb and
intimidate Stalin. Alperovitz often wrenches the meaning of secondary sources, and even documents, out of context.

Consider his citation of the diplomatic historian Gaddis Smith.
Alperovitz doesn't make clear which of Smith's works he is quot-

ing, but this is what Gaddis Smith says in the chapter entitled "The Bomb" in his standard work, *American Diplomacy During the Second World War:* "Stimson, Truman and their closest advisers believed that every question was subordinate to the necessity of ending the war as quickly and bloodlessly as possible. The bomb, despite its awful implications for the future of mankind, had to be considered first as a means toward that immediate end" (166). And: "Since the beginning of the year [1945] a peace party had been gaining influence with the [Japanese] cabinet, but the diehard views of the military leaders were still powerful in July, notwithstanding the fact that Japan's power for continued resistance was at an end" (168).

The latter, by the way, is a far from subtle distinction that Alperovitz and his disciples tend to miss when arguing that the bomb was not needed. Smith asks the key question: "Would the Japanese government have surrendered before the dropping of the bomb if the Potsdam Declaration had contained a clause permitting the retention of the Emperor? Probably not, if we assume that the bomb would have fallen on August 6. If we assume a double 'if': an assurance on the Emperor and the patience to hold back on the bomb while the Japanese cabinet went through the final agonies of debate, it does seem probable that Japan would have surrendered before many weeks had passed. . . . *But there is little profit in lingering too long over these might have beens"* (emphasis added). I find nothing in this familiar chapter of Gaddis Smith's book remotely resembling the contention that "the decision to bomb Japan was centrally connected," as Alperovitz puts it, "to Truman's confrontational approach to the Soviet Union." "Centrally connected"? "Confrontational approach"? The first phrase is evasive; the second is plainly contradicted by the fact that Smith, like most informed historians of the period, assumes good faith on Truman's part.

A more explicit refutation of Alperovitz's central accusation (or insinuation) is to be found in Herbert Feis's *The Atomic Bomb and the End of World War II*, pages 194–95. After reinvestigating the issue for the second edition of an earlier book, Feis once again concludes that the reckoning of the Allies was "governed by one reason deemed paramount: that by using the bomb the agony of war might be ended most quickly and lives be saved." Japan still had 3 million men under arms; Alperovitz and his acolytes don't bother to note the appalling damage done by the kamikazes during the Okinawa battle, nor the fact that Japan's stock of suicide planes and pilots was far from exhausted. More to the point, after speculating that Churchill and Truman perhaps "conceived," with Stimson and Byrnes, that the decision to use the bomb "would improve the chances of arranging a satisfactory peace both in Europe and in the Far East" by impressing the Russians and, as Feis puts it, "monitoring Russian behavior," he then continues: "Recognition of this element in official thinking must not be distorted into an accusation that the American government engaged in what Soviet propagandists and historians have called 'atomic blackmail.' To the contrary, even after the American government knew that it would have the supreme weapon, it keenly sought to preserve the friendly connection with the Soviet Union . . . [and] patiently sought compromise solutions for situations in dispute."

Here again is a distinction that Alperovitz glides over. Truman and his advisers would have had to be idiots not to assume that a temporary American monopoly of atomic weapons had dealt them a trump card, and not merely in the bloody task of bringing the Pacific war to an end. But, as Feis notes, it hardly follows that they thought it right or useful to make a swaggering display of the bomb in their diplomatic dealings, with Moscow or anyone else. The balanced views of Smith and Feis are echoed in dozens of places by other historians. In their totality, they constitute a withering repudiation of Alperovitz's suggestion that he speaks for a "new consensus." And they demolish that supposed "consensus" as well.

Perhaps the most cogent recent demolition of the revisionist "cult," as the author calls it, is in Robert Newman's *Truman and the Hiroshima Cult,* published while the *Enola Gay* argument was going full tilt. Newman, a professor of journalism at the University of Pittsburgh, documents the way in which revisionist views of Truman and the bomb originated in the tragic national dispute over Vietnam—as did so many other exotic perspectives on the generation who fought and won World War II and then designed American strategy for the cold war. The 1960s provided the seedbed for the view that the American motive in using atomic weapons against Japan was not to jolt the Japanese into surrender and save thousands of lives but to discourage Soviet geopolitical adventure in Europe.

That thesis, as Newman shows, required the wholesale rearrangement of many collateral details—the "discovery" that anticipated American and Allied casualty figures in an invasion of the Japanese home islands were greatly exaggerated; that the Japanese leaders were war weary and ready to quit, rather than, as was clearly the case, closely split between a peace party and a still powerful and impenitent military clique; that Harry Truman cold-bloodedly ignored Japanese peace feelers and refused to qualify the unconditional surrender demand when there was still time to do so; and that the United States used a "barbaric" weapon against Japan which it never would have used against Germany, reflecting the "racism" of American war policy. The revisionists seldom acknowledge how formidably the Japanese were fortifying Kyushu, preparing a defense that might well have made Okinawa (where more than twelve thousand Americans died) look like a picnic.

In fact, the great exercise in hindsight over the Hiroshima bombing looks, so far, to be more useful as a study of historians than of the history they write. History is too often conceived to be a gradual accumulation of certainties, mounting to a grand conclusion and, in this instance, resolving such questions as whether Japan might have surrendered promptly if the atomic weapons had not been used. History in that sense is now so blurred by polemics that consensus is beyond us. But we shall rarely have a better case study in how historians operate.

Consider the debate over the estimates of probable American casualties in the event that the war had continued beyond mid-August and that the scheduled Operation Olympic had been mounted in November. The estimates varied, and the variation, as Robert Newman has shown, was in part driven by service rivalries. The navy was keen to show that its blockade of Japan could win the war unaided. It therefore endorsed higher casualty estimates than prevailed in army circles. The estimates were also, as I noted earlier, driven by the frightening toll of the long battle for Okinawa, and extrapolations from it.

But whether high or low—and since the estimates were never tested in battle no one can say now whether the optimists or the pessimists were right—what ultimately mattered was not the accuracy of these projections but their psychological effect on the Allied war leaders, especially President Truman, Secretary of War Stimson and General Marshall, a point that seems to escape revisionist historians.

As the *Enola Gay* controversy raged, I was telephoned one day by a fellow journalist who was preparing a magazine piece about the controversy for a journalism quarterly. He had read several of my columns and wanted to know where I had obtained the estimate of a million casualties. "Much too high!" he commented, not explaining how he could possibly know. The figure, as I told him, is conventional. It had appeared in the public record by 1947, in Stimson's *Harper's Magazine* article "The Decision to Use the Atomic Bomb" and elsewhere. But a historian evaluating this or any other casualty estimate must recognize that it is the effect, not the accuracy, of the projection that matters. A parallel from the American Civil War comes to mind. It is well known that Gen. George B. McClellan, as commander of the Army of the Potomac during the Peninsula Campaign, grossly exaggerated the size of Robert E. Lee's opposing army. He did so in part because he was instinctively cautious, in part because Lee had gained the reputation of a military magician, and in part because McClellan's spies (Allan Pinkerton and others) fed him inflated figures which he in turn tended further to inflate.

Historically, which is the more significant factor—the "real" size of Lee's force, or the larger size McClellan attributed to it? Almost certainly the latter, since McClellan's chronic caution, even when he actually enjoyed an overwhelming tactical advantage, exasperated Lincoln and led him to sack McClellan not once but twice. Similarly, the evaluation of President Truman's motives in using the bombs depends far more on what he believed about the prospective toll in lives of invading Japan than on whether those fears were "realistic." Yet in their eagerness to portray Truman as a fool or war criminal, revisionist historians dwell on the conjecture that casualty estimates were exaggerated. So they may have been, but who can say?

For the first twenty years after Hiroshima, the view prevailed that Truman used the bomb to end the war and save lives—the view I still emphatically hold. Then something happened. It is often insinuated that the something was the discovery of new evidence, throwing new light on Truman's motives. In fact, what happened was this country's misadventure in Vietnam and the bitter divisions it produced. Those divisions nurtured a generation of historians who read their now-skeptical views back into the motives of the World War II leaders. Before the suspicion came to prevail that the American people were systematically deceived about Vietnam, it was easier for most people, and most historians, to accept at face value what leaders said about their decisions and motives. Historians now reflect a deepening cynicism. But it is the mood that changed, not the evidence, which in most respects remains as it was in 1961 when Herbert Feis wrote *Japan Subdued: The Atomic Bomb and the End of the War in the Pacific,* as the first edition was called. Whatever one believes about Hiroshima—and so violent and tragic an episode will of course be judged in a variety of ways—it should always be recalled that the motives and moods of historians are as essential to the understanding of the history they write as the motives and moods they attribute to the actors they write about.

Hitler and the Historians

IT IS A RARE student of history who is wholly free of nationalist bias, conscious or unconscious. But for half a century now, German historians have labored under a special burden. They can write almost nothing about the German past, near or remote, that does not in some way implicitly comment upon the lingering shadow of Adolf Hitler.

Hitler, born in the village of Branau, Austria, in April 1889, is certainly among the evildoers whose crib death would have spared the world much sorrow. For that reason as well as others, he continues to haunt the civilized imagination, in Germany and elsewhere, half a century after he died by his own hand in the Berlin bunker at the end of the war he started. To this day, his name and memory permit little more than ritual anathema. A storm of abuse greeted the suggestion of the British diplomatic historian A. J. P. Taylor (in his book *The Origins of the Second World War*) that, while Hitler exceeded all others in evil acts, his foreign policy was practically indistinguishable from that of the Weimar Republic and that he had blundered into an unintended war because Britain and France retreated every time he pushed a territorial claim.

In his novel *The Portage to San Cristobal of A. H.*, the critic George Steiner portrays Israeli commandos capturing a wizened Hitler in the Amazonian jungles. As they bring him back for the greatest of all war crimes trials, they are subjected to madcap seductive tirades whose gist it is that he—Hitler—should be honored as the founding father of modern Israel. Many readers were not amused; Hitler is no joking matter.

Can any detached truths be discerned amid the continuing argument about Hitler's historical significance? Perhaps one is that "great men"—even one whose magnitude lies in evildoing—do continue to shape history. It is a hard truth for our age, which is blinded by the tendency to sentimentalize the ordinary and extol the real—or imaginary—achievements of people en masse.

Great historical actors are almost always tormented by some compelling itch, for good or evil, frequently combined with a childish sense of insecurity or marginality. In Hitler's case, the contributing factors are easily pinpointed. He grew up in the border marches of the great, polyglot Austro-Hungarian empire, the son of an obscure imperial bureaucrat. His rustic bigotries were whetted by the half-baked chatter of the Viennese cafes he frequented as a bohemian art student. All sorts of ultra-nationalist drivel filled his ears and inflamed his imagination, the gist of it being that the real "German folk" were being drowned in a sea of Slavs, Jews and other alien and inferior types. A revival of racial energy and pride would include the reclamation of political and territorial entitlements rightly belonging to the Germans—especially "living room" to the east.

These sweepings of the Vienna cafes found their way into the pages of *Mein Kampf*, the book Hitler wrote while serving time in prison for street brawling in the 1920s. No reader could then foresee how swiftly the glib Austrian corporal would gain power by legal means, brilliantly manipulating those German establishment forces who clumsily tried to use him. From the pages of *Mein Kampf*, however, could be inferred much of his program of conquest.

No doubt the economic instability of Germany in the interwar years, her exclusion as a pariah from world counsels, helped advance Hitler's prospects. Without the inequities of the Versailles treaty, not even Hitler, incomparably the most incendiary demagogue of the century, could have gone so far. The peacemakers of 1919 are implicated in his mischief. Yet as the historian Hugh Trevor-Roper has argued, deterministic excuses for wars are rarely convincing. Yes, there were geographic "instabilities" (the inclusion of the German-speaking Sudetenland in the Czechoslovak state, the Polish corridor bisecting Germany); and there were economic grievances, including the steep reparations bills. But such factors do not necessarily provoke devastating wars. It is when a Hitler begins to put his visions into effect that, as W. B. Yeats wrote, "Things fall apart; the centre cannot hold;/ . . . The blood-dimmed tide is loosed, . . ."

And that brings me to the curiously evasive words that marked the fortieth observance of the end of the war Hitler started. Ronald Reagan, then president of the United States, and Mikhail Gorbachev, general secretary of the Soviet Communist Party, both engaged in some discreet doctoring of the credit lines for the defeat of Hitler.

Gorbachev's anniversary speech to the Supreme Soviet heaped blame for Hitler's rampage on the "Munich collusion," as he called it, the 1938 centerpiece of British Prime Minister Neville Chamberlain's appeasement policy (of which more below). The guarantors of Czechoslovakia's borders permitted Hitler to annex the Germanic borderlands without a fight, in the hope that this concession would sate his territorial appetite. In Gorbachev's doctored version, Munich was treated not as an act of folly by the democracies, but as a scheming attempt by "monopoly capital" to deflect Hitler's aggressions eastward. (As *Mein Kampf* had made clear, of course, Hitler needed no such deflection.) Gorbachev had nothing to say about the embarrassing fact that in 1939, a year after Munich, Stalin and Hitler signed a nonaggression pact at Poland's expense. Munich doubtless played a role, but the war started only after the Hitler-Stalin accord secured Hitler's eastern flank and enabled him to seize much of Poland and maraud Western Europe unmolested. This is an essential piece in the historical fabric of the century of which, before the collapse of the Soviet Union, young Russians heard little.

But then young Americans didn't learn much from Ronald Reagan's glowing picture of U.S. behavior and intentions about our own contributory negligence in the origins of World War II. The United States connived in nothing so malicious as the Hitler-Stalin pact. Our sin of omission was a sanctimonious standoffishness. The United States detached itself from the world with the usual claim that detachment is the reward of historical innocence. But the claim to innocence was as phony and self-deceiving as Gorbachev's doctored view of Munich.

The United States had involved itself irretrievably in the destiny of Europe by entering World War I in 1917. Once we plunged into that conflict, in defense of the rights of neutral shipping, we contributed our share to the destruction of the old European state system. To replace it, President Woodrow Wilson offered the idea of "self-determination," which implied that every distinct linguistic culture deserved a national identity. And, having introduced this intoxicating novelty, we became disillusioned at how hard it was to work out its practical consequences. We came home and slammed the door. Hitler was the primary beneficiary.

But while the foregoing reflections would seem to represent a certain consensus, there is a different theory for almost every historian or historical school. In his book *In Hitler's Shadow: West German Historians and the Attempt to Escape from the Nazi Past* (1987) the English historian Richard J. Evans argues that historical writing in Germany since the war has passed through three identifiable stages.

In the first, there was an embarrassed avoidance of the moral issues raised by Nazism, the origins of Hitler's aggressive policies, and his genocidal assault upon Jews, Slavs, Gypsies and other unfortunates. In this early period, German historians tended to take the literal-minded view that history is indeed "the past as it was," a chronicle of undisputed fact that speaks for itself and requires no interpretive gloss. In German schools under the benign aegis of

Chancellor Konrad Adenauer and his Christian Democratic colleagues, there was accordingly little or no confrontation with the Nazi past. It was a fact, but a fact about which Germans were left to draw their own personal conclusions.

Then came a second era with Willy Brandt and the Social Democrats, their political mood and moment heightened by the worldwide upheavals of the 1960s. The change of regimes, in which bridges tentatively began to be built with the other Germany on the other side of the Berlin wall, brought a flowering of inquiry into the implications of the Nazi past. It was stimulated by the mounting curiosity of a younger generation of Germans no longer content to be fobbed off with "the facts" and a wave of the hand. Explanations were demanded.

Still more recently, the return of the Christian Democrats to power under Chancellor Helmut Kohl and his coalition has brought on a more conservative mood. With that change, Evans believes, has come a resurgence of historical nationalism. The controversial Bitburg affair—Ronald Reagan's hurried ceremonial visit to a military cemetery where some former SS troopers were buried—was symptomatic. Among the latest urges, Evans writes, are attempts to "relativize" Hitler's crimes—not by denying them or minimizing their evil but by framing them in the perspective of other great twentieth-century atrocities, such as the Turkish massacre of Armenians during World War I and the recent bestialities of Pol Pot and the Khmer Rouge in Cambodia, or by comparing them to the monumental if different crimes of Stalin, or suggesting that they were a wicked but understandable response to the provocations of others.

Another persistent feature of the new revisionism—apart from crank denials that events such as the Holocaust occurred—is the portrayal of Hitler as a monstrous aberration, a leader whose style and politics find slight lineage or precedent in German history.

All of this has generated a fierce "battle of the historians," in which scholarly civilities are often forgotten. Evans views this resurgence of historical nationalism with concern and even muted alarm. In spite of his cautious and clinical approach, Evans's self-restraint wears thin. He has very strong personal views about German do-

mestic politics. He is very anti-Kohl. So it naturally emerges between the lines of his scholarly argument that there is, after all, a
correct view of the Hitler era: it is essential to see that Hitler, monster though he was, embodied certain familiar flaws in German political character—anti-Semitism, for instance. If he carried such
nativist obsessions to criminal and perverted lengths, still one may
detect echoes in those obsessions of an earlier Germany.

It follows that the new Germany, in Evans's view, would do well
to go on reminding itself of Hitler's continuities with the national
past, as well as his departures from it. Historians should not make
themselves parties to the antihistorical enterprise of "putting the
past behind us." The argument is persuasive. What is surprising is
that Evans seems unaware of the degree to which his personal views
about German politics govern and color his appraisal of the duties
of historians. Moreover, as Evans himself admits, the real problem
is that the demographic basis for German contrition and self-con-
sciousness about the Hitler past is wearing away. Most Germans
living today have no personal memory of the war or Hitler. They
may be keenly interested in the history of the 1933–45 era, but
understandably believe that they bear no personal responsibility.
The real division is over what inference is to be drawn from the
disappearance of the "guilty generation." The political right, represented by nationalist historians, says that it is time to assimilate the
problematic past, to set aside obsessions with hereditary or collective guilt. With equal plausibility and passion, the left insists that it
is dangerous to forget, to dismiss the special horrors of Nazi crimi-
nality or minimize its roots in the German past. Both are right, or
half right; both have a strong case.

Many of these old elements of the debate about Hitler and his historical legacy came together again in 1988 when the fiftieth anniversary of the Munich agreement was widely observed and its
continuing significance appraised. In that much-lamented episode
in late September of 1938, the leaders of Britain and France, as
guarantors of the integrity of Czechoslovakia, permitted Hitler to
do unresisted what he threatened to do by force: incorporate the
German-speaking Sudetenland into his Third Reich. Ever since, or

at least since the folly of the agreement came to be clearly understood, "Munich" has been a byword for calamitous diplomatic appeasement.

Certainly Munich has been thought to teach a variety of caution-
ary lessons. But how historical are they? Norman Podhoretz, the
editor of *Commentary* magazine, argued on the occasion of the fiftieth anniversary that the British had been "forced by their own
weakness" into a "humiliating capitulation." The balance of forces
in Europe, he suggested, had been shifting for five years or more
as Hitler defiantly rearmed Germany in violation of the Treaty of
Versailles. But it was not military weakness, so much as the fear of
war on any terms, that prompted the betrayal of Czechoslovakia.
Britain and France had the military power to stop Hitler. The
French were ready to fight, and so were the Czechs themselves.
Their army had been mobilized, and their fortifications in the Sude-
ten borderlands that Hitler proposed to seize were formidable. If
Hitler had attacked he probably would have been defeated and
then, very possibly, overthrown by his own generals. Several of
them, it seems, were horrified when the Allies yielded. The missing
element was not strength; it was will and clarity of vision.

Another misconception is that Hitler was still a mystery in
1938—or, as Podhoretz wrote, that he was not "widely perceived
as anything more than a conventional European statesman pursuing conventional national interests." This is a strange notion, perhaps a ghostly echo of A. J. P. Taylor's perverse argument (above)
that Hitler, though a very nasty man, was essentially pursuing traditional German foreign policies of the 1920s.

This idea will not bear historical scrutiny. Hitler's ambitions were
already considered by the farsighted, of whom there were a large
number, to be extravagant and menacing and his methods thug-
gish. He had already forcibly absorbed Austria into the Reich by
threat and fraud. Among those who saw through him, Winston
Churchill was the most outspoken. But there were others, including
the French prime minister, Daladier, and many British diplomats
and politicians: Sir Eric Phipps, the former ambassador to Berlin;
Robert Vansittart, permanent head of the Foreign Office; and, in
Parliament, Duff Cooper, Harold Nicolson, Julian Amery and oth-

ers of many political persuasions. The letters and diaries of the period show conclusively that all knew and said that Hitler was a
fanatic, his followers hoodlums, his ambitions fraught with war.
Their views were neither unheard nor disregarded. They were over-
ridden by wishful thinking and—again—the fear of war. There was
nothing "conventional" about Hitler, and only the self-deluded
claimed there was. The truth is that Norman Podhoretz, one of the
old liberals who supported Ronald Reagan in 1980, has found in
the lessons of Munich a handy ratification of his own recent views
on U.S. defense policy.

If England and France had the power to stop Hitler in 1938, and
if Hitler's character was clear, why then the capitulation at Munich?
Three explanations suggest themselves, of many. There was above
all the fear that war would renew the slaughter which all European
states had endured only twenty years earlier. There was the Ger-
manophilia of the squires and businessmen—at least the more wit-
less among them—who formed the backbone of the British
Conservative Party. It was augmented by their fear of Russia and
of communism. It wasn't an Englishman who said "Better Hitler
than Blum" (i. e., better Nazism than the popular front coalition of
the left formed by the French socialist Leon Blum), but many in
England as well as France thought it. And finally there was an un-
pardonable indifference to the interests of a small but functioning
new nation whose stubbornness seemed to threaten the peace: "a
faraway place, of which we know little," as Chamberlain said.

If you translate these elements into what we like to call historical
lessons, they might be phrased as follows: don't allow present policy to be paralyzed by shaky analogies drawn from the past. Remember that nationalist prejudices—Russophobia in this
instance—can cloud judgment. And don't assume that you will gain
in the long run by dishonoring solemn commitments when they
become inconvenient and dangerous.

While such rules are frequently broken, the truth is that reading
lessons into past events, though often deplored, is not only appropriate; it is inescapable. In that sense, most of us heed Lord Acton's
famous charge to the student historians of Cambridge University
more than a century ago. In his inaugural lecture as Regius Profes-

sor of Modern History in June 1895, he exhorted his audience "never to debase the moral currency or to lower the standard of rectitude, but to try others by the final maxim that governs your own lives, and to suffer no man and no cause to escape the undying penalty which history has the power to inflict on wrong. . . . At every step we are met by arguments which go to excuse, to palliate, to confound right and wrong, and reduce the just man to the level of the reprobate."

What Lord Acton said is undeniable, but he said it at a time far less haunted by ambiguities and complexities than the twentieth century has proved to be. Hitler makes an easy target for "the undying penalty which history has the power to inflict on wrong," and there is no danger that the great reprobate will ever be raised to the level of the just. The more difficult challenge lies in assessing the wisdom of policies that seemed to ratify his gangster-like behavior.

Of the latter, Munich has for more than half a century seemed to the world a paramount example. The Munich analogy became an axiom of post–World War II statecraft: concessions made to aggressors at gunpoint do not avoid conflict; they invite further aggression. When confronted by Josef Stalin's evident drive for political dominance in eastern and central Europe in the late 1940s, the generation who had fought the Second World War consulted Munich for guidance and decided that resistance, not concession, would be the rule—up to a point, at least, for no one wished to ignite a nuclear war. The case of Adolf Hitler proves that historians are instinctive moralists; for judgment is the inescapable essence of historical inquiry. The trick is to be wary of the tinctures of personal prejudice that affect what we think and say of the events and figures of the past, and to make sure that we do not distort the lessons of history with wishful or present-minded thinking.

Micronations and the
Force of Nationalism

WE AMERICANS ARE rarely noted for patient familiarity with the little anomalies of history and geography—not even our own. But these anomalies always matter to someone, somewhere. With the disintegration of the Soviet Union in the early 1990s, the Baltic republics reasserted the national independence they had lost in 1939. George McGhee, the former undersecretary of state and ambassador to Germany, told me that when Lithuania began agitating for restored independence he looked up "Lithuania" in the *Encyclopedia Britannica* and found that in the past the Lithuanians had pushed the Russians around for longer than the Russians had returned the favor.

When, for related reasons, secessionist fever swept over the principalities of Yugoslavia in 1991, the Bush administration was much berated for ignoring American political ideals. How? By officially supporting, with reservations, the "territorial integrity" of the Yugoslav federal state as it had existed since World War I. The critical comments of Jeane J. Kirkpatrick were typical—and, in hindsight, impulsive. The former U.S. ambassador to the United Nations wrote in her newspaper column regarding Yugoslav secessionism: "Americans and their government should prefer self-determination to territorial integrity as a political value. . . . Government by consent is a right of person. Territorial integrity is an attribute of states."

It was a typical academic formulation; unfortunately, the wreckage secessionism made of "government by consent" in the ensuing tragic years of "ethnic cleansing" and other horrors suggested that knowing a bit of history can be useful.

Perhaps it is my Confederate ancestry, but Kirkpatrick's suggestion that "self-determination" is the overriding political value of the American experience prompted me to wonder: since when? All these years, I had been conditioned at the knee of my historical mentors to believe that "self-determination" was more or less what South Carolina, Mississippi, Alabama and other rebellious southern states sought in 1861—and that it was the wrong sort. If the hot-headed fire-eaters had left Fort Sumter alone, who knows what the upshot might have been? America might be two nations today—or a dozen. When secession fever intensified after the election of Abraham Lincoln in late 1860, in the mistaken belief that a Lincoln presidency meant an assault on slavery, scores of constitutionalists thought that secession, however deplorable, was perfectly legal. Horace Greeley, the famous *New York Tribune* editor, thought so. "Let the erring sisters depart in peace," he said.

In the long run, unionism was preferable. But my point here is that forgetting alternative possibilities and ironies in history—even our own—has become a fertile source of American arrogance. We tend to lecture errant multitudes abroad on the virtue of our example, though the example we have in mind is often fictitious. Our great historical myth, our pattern and paradigm for judging all that is right and righteous, is the great morality play of 1776—thirteen oppressed colonies, unjustly taxed without parliamentary representation, rebelling against George III. This primal myth was later elaborated, made into a blueprint for the cure of all European ills, by Woodrow Wilson's Fourteen Points. On the wings of that great manifesto, we soared off in 1917 to make the world safe for democracy—on the basis, indeed, of "self-determination." Still today, a blend of the Declaration of Independence and the Fourteen Points forms our template for judging the correctness of political alignments elsewhere.

The dissolution of Yugoslavia after nearly three-quarters of a century of federated life certainly involved self-determination of a tragic and unmanageable complexity. As we saw in the cruel civil war in Bosnia, it involved the displacement of ethnic minorities trapped among majorities. This is an endemic and potentially explosive problem all across eastern and southeastern Europe—the dilemma of ethnic Russians in Lithuania and Georgia, of ethnic Serbs in Croatia and Bosnia, indeed of Hungarians in Slovakia. In the years when Marshal Tito held Yugoslav together, personal inclination and opportunity led to much internal migration, accompanied by a healthy forgetfulness of ethnicity, as it does in all federal states. It is very hard to unscramble an egg on the basis of a simpleminded slogan like self-determination.

The Bush administration was right—not that it made much difference—to remind the Yugoslavs of an earlier and better American idea: James Madison's idea of the "extended republic," in which central and local bodies share authority, and the clash of ethnic interests and nationalist memories is softened by common laws and a central judiciary strong enough to vindicate individual rights. That is a better model for the future of southeastern Europe than the rash eruption of frisky microstates. When South Carolina seceded 136 years ago, a distinguished unionist of that state scoffed that it was "too small to be a nation and too large to be an insane asylum." In these interdependent times, that goes as well for a number of would-be secessionist states all around the periphery of Europe.

I take no great satisfaction in having questioned, a bit earlier than most observers, that the end of the cold war and of the great power rivalry with the Soviet Union that had marked it for forty years would ring in a millennium of tranquillity. I claim no special foresight, only the belief that knowing even a little history is the best guide to the present. Anyone who had read very far into the history of nineteenth- and twentieth-century Europe might have feared, as proved to be the case, that the end of the cold war would stimulate a resurgence of tribal nationalism and all the bloody rivalries that go with it—most intensively in those places where the pressure of ideology and great power rivalry had suppressed ethnic aspirations for a generation and longer. Yugoslavia was typical, but Yugoslavia is not alone.

There is, of course, a more complicated way to view these struggles, now that we have been whisked, as if in an H. G. Wells time machine, from the nuclear dangers and "bipolar" world of 1988 back to the nationalist dangers of—when?—1912? When I studied nineteenth-century European history at Oxford forty years ago, my tutors insisted that I attempt a meticulous, if temporary, mastery of that bewildering patchwork of petty nationalities (as many as nineteen in all, if you credit that master counter, Sir Lewis Namier), without which the turmoil of those allegedly simpler times made no sense. If you aspired to understand what Prussia's iron chancellor, Otto von Bismarck, had meant when he declared that the "eastern question" wasn't worth the bones of a Pomeranian grenadier, or the nature of the so-called "Turkish atrocities" in Greek areas ruled from Constantinople that stirred the high indignation of William E. Gladstone's Liberal cabinets, or what fissures and fractures were at play in the Austro-Hungarian empire, you had to know a Bosnian from a Slovene and a Serb from a Croat. I fondly imagined, back then, that once I had satisfied the learned examiners and returned to the simplicities of the New World, I need never recall those tangled matters again. But there I was mistaken. These fissures haven't vanished; they have simply been in hiding.

It now begins to appear that many forgotten nationalisms, and the linguistic, religious and territorial passions that fuel them, were merely slumbering in unquiet graves, awaiting the disintegration of the Soviet Union to rise again. All this, however, seems to have come as a shock to many Americans. We had the good fortune to experience our own adolescent age of "manifest destiny" in an empty continent, inhabited by a few tribes of noble savages and militarily inferior Mexicans, oblivious to the romantic nationalism that swept Europe at the time of the French Revolution. It is evidently one of our prejudices that things historical and geographical, once fixed, ought to stay fixed. Our own brief flirtation with secessionism and multinational identity failed, and the failure was accepted. As the Balkans and other realms of unresolved nationalist tension renew their ancient tendency to fly to pieces, we are inclined either to dismiss them (do we really care what happened to Serbs at the battle of Kosovo a thousand years ago?) or to measure their merits by the Wilsonian formula of self-determination.

There was great consternation when, one day in the early 1990s, the deputy secretary of state, Lawrence Eagleburger, mused in a speech at Georgetown University that the end of the cold war might bring some momentary distress. Say what one might of its negative aspects, which were frightening indeed, the cold war relationship between the two great superpowers gradually came to be characterized by considerable stability—a style of managing unsettling contingencies, rather like the balance of power system of the age of Metternich. It exhibited the features of a developed state system. Eagleburger, though he didn't put it exactly that way, spoke no less than the truth. He was impetuously and scornfully attacked for expressing "nostalgia," it was said, for the cold war. That was the gist of a silly speech or two in the United States Senate, and more than one silly newspaper column, soon to be echoed by the usual camp followers on network television. But Eagleburger's meaning was mistaken. He was merely saying what is obvious—that when the world is locked in a global confrontation, and when that is the pattern to which all lesser conflicts are subordinated, it does simplify the task of statesmen—not that it makes their task easier. Conversely, when the confrontation ceases, things may become far more complicated, for the mice will play.

So where do we stand now? Who really owns what piece of real estate in central Europe, and who will write the ultimate deed on the basis of what definitive geopolitical title search? Now that Lithuanians have regained their independence, will Poland ask to have its historic slice of Lithuania? If that slice were given back, would the Poles then repent of the Oder-Neisse line and, in a fit of generosity, hand Silesia and Pomerania back to a reunited Germany driven from those old Germanic lands in 1944–45? And if the Germans regained East Prussia, might they. . . ? If one asks questions of this sort—and of course they are implicitly asked every time some ancient nationalist claim is dusted off—where does it end? As in any crowded neighborhood, every deed and quitclaim implicates every other. At the time of the English civil war, those primitive egalitarians, the Levelers, liked to ask:

> When Adam delved, and Eve span,
> Who was then the gentleman?

The point was that at some perhaps imaginary stage of remote prehistory, well before lords and ladies and courts and thrones and sumptuary laws were ever thought of, everyone must have existed in a state of natural equality. But that radical egalitarianism has rarely commended itself as a useful basis for dividing the spoils and privileges of human society—not, at least, outside the fictive realm of Sir Thomas More's Utopia. No more, I imagine, can civilization rest easy upon a kind of infinitely regressive quarrel over nationalistic titles and rights. I take comfort here from Sir Lewis Namier, one of the greatest of twentieth-century historians, who, in commenting on the tangle of nineteenth-century European nationalist rivalries, advised: "I refrain from inquiring into the sense of the envenomed struggles we have witnessed; for such inquiry would take us into inscrutable depths or into an airy void. Possibly there is no more sense in human history than in the changes of the seasons or the movements of the stars; or if sense there is, it escapes our penetration."

Bleak but sensible counsel. Namier went on to argue that the best to be hoped for, taking the historical view, is a grasp of the inner logic of events. For me at least, the key to that logic is that when dynasties and empires die, as they have been doing steadily for the past half century or so, including now at long last the Soviet empire, an age of agitated minuscule nationalities may well follow. Unfortunately, that development hardly signals the coming of an age of peace and harmony. That we should be surprised at this is the real surprise. Namier was a well of fascinating insights, perhaps because he was himself a central European by birth and heritage, even though his adopted nation was England. Here he is, for instance, on the subject of Prince Metternich, the architect of the "reactionary" system of dynastic legitimacy that the Congress of Vienna introduced in 1815, following the ravages of Napoleon: "Conservatism, of which Metternich was an exponent, is primarily based on a proper recognition of human limitation. . . . The history of the French Revolution and Napoleon had shown once more the immense superiority which existing social forms have over human movements and genius. . . . It was the greatness and strength of Metternich during those fateful years to have foreseen that human contrivances . . . however clever and beneficial, would not endure, and to have understood the peculiar elasticity with which men would finally revert to former habits. The failure of striving, struggling men brings the heir of the ages back into his own."

Indeed, if there is value in musing at this late date upon the upheavals of the end of the twentieth century, it is to be found, once again, in Namier's historical wisdom—in the "peculiar elasticity" (wonderful phrase) of human political habit that so often confounds idealistic arrangements. Americans remain incurably optimistic that history's "peculiar elasticity" may safely be disregarded. Woodrow Wilson, or those who drafted his Fourteen Points, thought in the winter of 1918 that "the system of the balance of power" had been "forever discredited." They were wrong. The Wilsonian vision of self-determination prevailed for a time. The old transnational empires nursed in their old age by Metternich and his associates had collapsed and were contemptuously discarded. In their place rose many small, independent states built upon the artifice of linguistic nationalism and "self-determination." Within twenty brief years, however, a fraction of the lifetime of Metternich's system, more ruthless and despotic states, invoking exactly the same nationalistic slogans in a cynical and fraudulent way, were preying upon these independent peoples, and they lacked the strength and unity to resist. It is difficult to conclude from this that Metternich, in his suspicion of nationalist fervors, was either a villain or a fool, still less a failure. I entertain the haunting view that his statecraft will endure, for the reasons Namier states so eloquently, when less historically grounded ideas of political organization have vanished.

Yalta in History and Myth

No survey of the crossroads between past and present can be complete without a glance at the distortion of history for partisan purposes. For Americans of my vintage, the crowning instance was what was made for several decades of the Yalta conference of February 1945. There, at the old czarist winter resort in the Crimea, the "Big Three" of World War II, Roosevelt, Churchill and Stalin, settled outstanding matters for the last phase of their wartime alliance. There were two great issues at Yalta, and they were linked: the political and geographical future of Poland and the defeat of Japan.

Throughout the cold war years, "Yalta"—the word alone—became a party slogan. On Republican lips, any mention of Yalta—a "sellout," as it was routinely described—was calculated to remind American voters of Polish ancestry that Franklin D. Roosevelt had allegedly abandoned democratic Poland to Stalin's clutches.

As if Nemesis had finally turned the tables, the issue of Poland became a stumbling block for the Republicans in the 1976 presiden-

tial election, when Jimmy Carter challenged Gerald R. Ford. In a
television debate between the two candidates, Ford embraced the
bizarre view that the Poles were "free" and did not consider themselves to be under Soviet domination. The assertion was so startling
a departure from the usual Republican congressional rhetoric
(which had long listed Poland among the "captive nations" of central Europe) that Max Frankel of the *New York Times*, one of the
panel of journalists questioning the candidates, offered Ford an opportunity to modify the remark. Did he really mean to say what he
seemed to be saying? Frankel asked. Ford declined to qualify or
temper the remark. It was soon being depicted as a capital blunder.

The story of Ford's remark, and of his stubborn refusal to dilute
it, though not widely known, is one of the fascinating footnotes, if
no more, of American election history. Not long after Ford succeeded the disgraced Richard Nixon in the summer of 1974, a controversy arose in the Washington press over a briefing the State
Department counselor, Helmut Sonnenfelt, had given in London
for American diplomats from various European postings. Henry
Kissinger, then Ford's secretary of state, was regarded on the Republican right as the architect of "detente" with the Soviet Union,
and Sonnenfelt was identified in the same quarters as Kissinger's
right-hand man. His remarks in London, of which the only author-
itative version consisted of notes taken by Warren Zimmermann,
an experienced foreign service officer, were depicted as an echo of
Kissingerian cynicism. Sonnenfelt's talk (and, by implication, Kissinger's detente policy) was portrayed as a gesture of appeasement
of Soviet imperial claims and support of the status quo in Poland
and elsewhere. It was no such thing; its main thrust, a matter of
simple common sense, was that it would be better for European
peace and stability if the Soviet Union sought a more normal, less
coercive, relationship with its so-called "satellites," Poland and
Hungary in particular.

Before the debate with Carter, Ford had been strictly advised to
insist, at the earliest opportunity, that the United States recognized
no such Soviet claim to suzerainty over the nations of eastern Europe, certainly not Poland. Ford's artless attempt to stick to his
script explained the strange remark about Poland, which as he

stated it seemed far removed from reality. It triggered all the old feelings about Poland as a "captive nation," and Ford was soon hounded into one of those highly visible processes of self-correction that can do so much damage in modern television campaigns. And in a way, the Democrats at last had their revenge for a generation's taunting about Yalta. The episode was full of historical ironies.

No one who recalls the long life of the "Yalta" warcry in American party politics imagined in 1976 that within a decade of Ford's blunder, Poland would indeed be reasserting her political independence under the leadership of the shipyard workers of Gdansk— formerly the free city of Danzig, which in the 1930s had been among Adolf Hitler's excuses for his bullying foreign policy. By then, Ford had lost an election, and so, in turn, had his successor Jimmy Carter.

At Stalin's insistence, the Polish boundaries established after the First World War were shifted westward in 1945—risking, as Churchill wittily said, stuffing the Polish goose too full of German sausage. The Curzon Line, far west of the borders of prewar Poland, became the eastern boundary with the Soviet Union. Serious historical studies of the Yalta agreements—notably, Robin Edmonds's book, *The Big Three*—have emphasized the slight leverage available to Roosevelt and Churchill as they sought to protect Polish interests in their chess game with Stalin, while simultaneously bidding for Soviet help in the defeat of Japan. Certainly it was tragic irony that a war declared in 1939 in keeping with an Anglo-French guarantee of Poland's borders (though having far larger and deeper causes) ended with the delivery of Poland from Nazi conquest to the control of Stalinist puppets.

As the conferees assembled at Yalta, Europe was hardly a lump of clay for molding. It was in chaos, a "charnel house," as Churchill would later write, of fleeing refugees, erased national borders, marching armies, the skeletal ruins of great cities, and disintegrating societies. In that setting, the insistence by Roosevelt and Churchill on guarantees of democratic elections in postwar Poland was, however genuine or well meant, built on sand. Stalin's armies already occupied Poland, and in these adverse circumstances it was remarkable that the Anglo-Americans labored as hard as they did for Polish independence. Presumably, they did assume some good faith on Stalin's part, and it was not altogether without foundation. In regard to Greece, for instance, Stalin would keep his word to Churchill that British influence would remain paramount there. That was in accord with historic practice. He did not recognize, however, the same degree of British or American interest in Poland. These were the historical realities.

In a notable fortieth-anniversary article on Yalta in the journal *Foreign Affairs*, Zbigniew Brzezinski, the former national security adviser to President Carter, observed that Allied solicitude for Poland was more emphatic at Yalta than it had been fifteen months earlier, at the Teheran conference. The missing factor, ignored even by Dr. Brzezinski, the loyal son of Polish patriots, was the overriding preoccupation of the Americans and British with the end of the war in the Pacific, which was expected to be bloody. The defeat of Hitler had had first priority. Once that was accomplished, a costly endgame with Japan was anticipated. It was expected that great sacrifices of life would be required to obtain the "unconditional surrender" of the Japanese home islands.

For that reason, Roosevelt and Churchill were overwhelmingly concerned to gain Stalin's participation. They did not then foresee the role of the atomic bomb or its decisive use at Hiroshima and Nagasaki. Its test at Alamagordo was still six months away, and the Americans would not venture to disclose its existence to the Russians until after the test had proved it a success, and then only indirectly at the Potsdam conference following the German surrender. Placing Yalta in that context does not excuse miscalculations about Poland's future, if such they were. It does show how pointless and contemptible it was to depict the Yalta agreement as if Roosevelt and Churchill had all the leverage in the world but declined to use it.

What alternatives were there, after all? To revoke or modify the "unconditional surrender" formula, so that the war with Japan could come to a negotiated end? After Pearl Harbor? To send Gen. George Patton bolting beyond his supply base to Prague, and a further deep penetration of what was to become the Russian sphere, then to try conclusions with huge Soviet land armies well to the east? That, after the German breakthrough in the Ardennes in December 1944 had so seriously disrupted the reinvasion of the continent? These are the possibilities that enthrall armchair strategists well after the fact, but in the battlefield conditions of the late winter of 1945 they ranged from unrealistic to unthinkable.

And even armchair strategists know that Poland, the alleged victim of betrayal at Yalta, has suffered from intractable historical adversities for centuries, largely because of her geographical exposure. The Poles had the misfortune as a nation to occupy much of the great north-European plain across which more powerful invaders, German or Russian or French, had passed to and fro from Napoleon to Hitler.

That it was within the power of Roosevelt and Churchill to overlook these conditions of history, strategy and fortune at the time was always a fantasy, born of exploitative ethnic politics, and unhistorical to the point of hubris. In historical terms, Yalta was the last great accord for some forty years of the two great isolationist powers, the United States and the Soviet Union, which had emerged (or been forced) from their isolation and stood at the high tide of arbitrary power. Everyone else was beaten or exhausted, but Stalin and Roosevelt commanded vast, restless and energetic armies which Europe, east or west, was powerless to check. Either could indulge an innocent belief in the power of ideas, democratic or revolutionary, to manhandle history and settle the affairs of mankind. Both Roosevelt the idealist and Stalin the cynic did so, but Stalin's expectations in Poland were the more realistic.

When George Bush and Mikhail Gorbachev met at Malta in 1989, to ratify the end of the cold war, the garrulous spokesman for the Soviet Foreign Ministry, Gennadi Gerasimov, proposed "from Yalta to Malta" as the theme of the meeting. Europe almost visibly shuddered, since it remained the view of many Europeans, as it had been of Republican politicians, that the Big Three had casually juggled national destinies like absentee landlords sorting the claims of their tenants. That was far from the case, for reasons discussed above, but during the Malta meeting it was more than once said, in the breathless shorthand of television news, that Yalta had been the place where Stalin "gained eastern Europe" or was presented with it on a platter by Churchill and Roosevelt. The fact is that Stalin's armies already had Poland by 1945.

At Yalta, Stalin was supporting the idea of a dismembered Germany and heavy reparations. He demanded, and professed to deserve, a friendly Poland. The United States had vaguely supported both ideas, favored by certain leftists in Washington, but as the Western Allies began to fear that a dismembered Germany would leave a dangerous vacuum in Europe, they started to hedge. In hindsight, neither the United States nor the Soviet Union had as much influence to exercise over the German or Polish future as either supposed. Those futures took many decades to assert themselves, but, with the decline of Soviet military power (or the will to use it as brutally as it had been used in 1956 and 1968) diversity has returned to these historic lands.

The event that signaled the beginning of the end of the long Soviet domination of Poland came when Mikhail Gorbachev, not long after assuming power in Moscow, permitted Russian collaboration in a joint Russian-Polish inquiry into the Katyn Forest massacres. The joint commission established the long-suppressed truth, which was that Stalin had ordered the execution of hundreds of Polish officers, and managed to pin that hideous and expedient war crime on the Germans. And Katyn was perhaps the most important influence at Yalta. It had been, after all, the strong Polish suspicion of the terrible truth about Katyn that prompted the Polish government in exile in London to stiffen its back towards Moscow, and by default to concede de facto control of Poland's fate to Stalin's puppet government at Lublin. This alone sufficed to complicate the already difficult task of Roosevelt and Churchill at Yalta. When the truth about Katyn was finally acknowledged more than four decades later, a long chain of fateful historical events came to closure. And so, at long last, did the cheap exploitation of high strategy in World War II for votes.

New Thoughts about
an Old Villain

~

THE SPANISH CIVIL WAR of 1936–39 deeply scarred the soul of an age. Small wonder, then, that its legacy, like King Charles II of England, is a long time a-dying. Yet dying it is, as any visitor to the vibrant post-Franco Spain discovers. Juan Pablo Fusi's *Franco* and Stanley G. Payne's *The Franco Regime: 1936–1975,* both published in 1987, the tenth anniversary of the post-Franco Spanish constitution, are among the signs that scholarly consideration of Francisco Franco's forty-year reign is now passing from the realm of polemic into the more measured realm of history.

The emerging spectacle is paradoxical. The man whose ascendancy stretched from the victory of the insurgents in 1936 to his quiet if painful death in bed in November 1975 (with the mummified arm of Saint Teresa of Avila at his side) was physically small and, to most eyes, unprepossessing. Francisco Franco was a soldier with strong but simple ideas—a Bonapartist, Stanley Payne suggests, without the genius of Bonaparte. He ruled a brilliant and volatile, and changing, society less by means of ideology than by means of traditionalist social convictions, and by a talent for agile accommodation. Even more than Louis XIV might Franco have boasted, "I am the state." His "organic Catholic democracy," as he liked to call it, was among the more durable political entities of the twentieth century. Yet it was also a system of jerry-built institutions that largely collapsed at his death.

From the time of his consolidation of power amid the ruins of the civil war in 1939 to his dying day, Franco claimed that he had rescued Spain from its familiar demons—"the spirit of anarchy, carping mutual criticism, lack of fellow-feeling, extremism, and internecine hatred," as he himself catalogued these faults in 1966. These chronic Spanish vulnerabilities (as Franco viewed them) offered Spain sinister temptations. There was communism, first and foremost; as late as 1943, Franco was offering to send a million volunteers to defend Berlin in the event of a Soviet breakthrough. Then, there was the supposed international Masonic conspiracy, which so obsessed Franco that he anonymously wrote and published a book about its machinations. He alone claimed to be able to steer Spain between the treacherous whirlpools of secular modernism and liberal democracy, on the one hand, and Marxist tyranny on the other. Thus Franco as viewed by Franco.

But the great question for historians now is the durability of the "ism" Franco founded. His Spanish biographer Juan Pablo Fusi and the American historian Stanley Payne largely agree about this. Franco, a general at thirty-three, had distinguished himself as a soldier. He was prudent and cautious and, as his shifting international associations showed, flexible and agile. Far from soft, he was, however, a man of cordiality and courtesy, unpretentious and averse to violence. By even conservative estimates, his regime executed some twenty-eight thousand to thirty thousand political enemies in the post–civil war years. That is a considerable butcher's bill for any revolution. Yet, as Fusi puts it, "Franco, who was not a violent man by temperament, applied the policy of repression dispassionately . . . as if fulfilling a duty." He was not a hater.

Francoism suffered from first to last from what Fusi calls "a kind of chronic sickness of conscience about the legitimacy of its origins." Without the early aid of Hitler and Mussolini, Franco's July

18, 1936, revolt might not have succeeded. German and Italian planes ferried his armies from their bases in Spanish Morocco to the mainland to launch his crusade against the divided and collapsing Second Republic. Well into the World War II years, Franco pursued an unsavory courtship of the fascist powers, a defect that saw Spain excluded from the United Nations. Ostracism began to fade only with the onset of the cold war, as Franco's self-advertised status as the aboriginal anti-Communist ("Sentinel of the West," in the phrase of one fawning biography) assumed a new pertinence. The American alliance, a new concordat with Rome and United Nations membership followed.

Franco's relationship with the deposed Spanish monarchy was abrasive, small help in legitimizing his claims. In his Rome Manifesto at the end of the Second World War, Don Juan, the Bourbon pretender, condemned Francoism as "inspired from its inception by the totalitarian system of the Axis powers." Franco protested, with some justice, that he had never been a fascist. As both Fusi and Payne show, the label is not precise—few political and ideological labels are. Both books, Payne's especially, show that attempted taxonomies of Franco's regime soon become mind-numbing exercises in political nominalism. In the post–Vatican II years, the 1960s and after, there came a sharp shift in the attitudes of the Catholic Church, whose guardian and servant Franco had always claimed to be above all else. The church hierarchy in Spain joined the shadow opposition. Franco resisted the blandishments of die-hard advisers and sought in pained silence to accommodate the church's advice.

Apart from its quest for moral legitimacy—for an escape from its reputation as what Payne calls "principal ogre of the Western world"—the other great Francoist problem was a search for institutionalization. Franco never accepted the rationale of liberal institutions—parties, trade unions, free press, free speech. He regarded them as poison for Spain and Spaniards. Yet a halting and furtive accommodation had to be made to an increasingly dynamic urban and industrial society, and made it was, often in evasive and comically hypocritical forms. Institutionally speaking, Francoism gradually became a study in anomaly and denial. Even when Franco's silent acquiescence in modern economic theory touched off (or released) the great boom of the 1960s and 1970s, Franco claimed to believe that prosperity merely vindicated the genius of his "organic" system.

Last among the major issues of Francoism was the succession, the question of whether Francoism would survive Franco. The Caudillo remained a man of robust health to the threshhold of his ninth decade. But a freak hunting accident in 1961 showed that he was mortal and crystalized the issue. Franco dithered for seven years over the succession, finally designating as his heir Prince Juan Carlos, the son of his old Bourbon critic. But Juan Carlos's succession at Franco's death was not to be a "restoration," the old dictator decreed; it would be an "instauration," a clean break with the liberal monarchy of the past that Franco blamed for many of Spain's ancient political difficulties. Franco hoped that Juan Carlos would preserve the forms, or at least the memory, of Francoism, but in the event he did not. He proved to be his father's son, a democrat and a constitutionalist.

The judgments of Franco and Francoism that emerge from both these recent books are incisive but measured. Recent revisionist historians of the Franco years are beginning to detect continuities that had been obscured by the bitter polemics and recriminations of Franco's lifetime. As Payne notes, it is arguable that Franco, for all his faults, played midwife to a transformed Spain that is today both more harmonious and politically stable—and free, by the measures of liberal democracy—than the Spain he seized in 1936. Had liberal democracy ever before been a realistic alternative? In the Spain of the depression years, an angrily polarized right and left, having crushed the moderate center, were bent on mutual destruction. It is also true, however, as Fusi writes, that "Franco established . . . a personal dictatorship which lasted for forty years and which by its very existence evoked revulsion." Those were in many respects lost years for Spain. A regime bidding for history's laurels must exhibit more than passive and defensive virtues, and it needs more than the shadowy demons that inhabited Franco's imagination to justify that defensiveness. Perhaps the best to be said of Franco and his ism today is that the Caudillo's passing left his successors poised to scrap his legacy and return, with renewed hope, to an older liberal tradition.

The foregoing assessment of the new histories of the Franco era appeared in a somewhat different form in the *Washington Post*'s Sunday book supplement in May 1988, following by a few months a delightful week in Madrid. My friend A. E. Dick Howard, professor of constitutional law at the University of Virginia, had been invited by an old student, Enrique Alonso Garcia, now an eminent Spanish academician, to help celebrate the U. S. bicentennial at the Instituto de Espagna. The observance would conveniently coincide with the decennial of Spain's post-Franco constitution. Howard and an associate of his choosing (it turned out to be me) were to deliver four lectures on the U. S. Constitution. We did so, Howard and I meanwhile keeping the engaging company of many of the dynamic spirits who had guided post-Franco Spain into the new era. Little was said during our visit about the darker years after the civil war, but little had to be. A journalist who takes a trip automatically becomes an authority, and friends at Book World, knowing of my journey, asked me to appraise several new books on the Franco era.

When my appraisal appeared, Robert Novak, the columnist and right-wing television sage, telephoned to tease me. "Yoder," he asked, "when you were a good little southern liberal growing up in North Carolina, did you ever for a moment imagine that you might someday say a good word for Francisco Franco?" I had to admit that I hadn't, and was frankly surprised to be doing so.

Novak, who masks a scholarly temperament behind the pose of a punditorial curmudgeon, put his finger on another of the surprising teases of history. We can't be sure in the short term what strange twists a story may take. The stock of an old hero may sink or that of an old villain may rise, all unexpectedly. In my youth Franco was regarded as but a shade less wicked than his three monstrous contemporaries, Stalin, Hitler and Mussolini. That was the conventional wisdom, though stock pictures no doubt oversimplified Franco's Iberian complexity. After all, George Orwell had warned us in his great book *Homage to Catalonia* that rights and wrongs, mercies and outrages, were bewilderingly mixed on both sides in the Spanish civil war. What could we fathom of the passionate enmities that divided the extremes of the Spanish clerical right from the extremes of the anticlerical and Marxist left, enmities having little counterpart in the clement politics of the English-speaking democracies? Maybe we deserve to be surprised when Spanish historians, taking a fresh look at the Franco period, speculate that Spain may in some ways have benefited from the respite Franco provided, with his authoritarian rule, from the passionate excesses of the thirties.

It has been said by another Iberian sage that "God writes straight with crooked lines," the favorite saying of a friend of mine. He applies it in a surprising fashion: had the heroic 1944 assassination plot of certain German officers, led by Claus von Stauffenberg and others, succeeded, Hitler's death and the replacement of the Nazis by a democratic government might perversely have sown the seeds of yet another legend that Germany had not really been defeated but, as in 1918, was betrayed by a "stab in the back." The words would seem also to fit the story of the crusty generalissimo who is now in retrospect beginning to be regarded by some historians as the unwitting midwife of a new and more democratic Spain. We could detect the crooked lines all along. It was only later that they could be seen as deviations from a transcendent pattern in which an older tradition of Spanish liberalism would ultimately be vindicated.

George F. Kennan and the
Follies of History

∾

THE HISTORY OF the early cold war years—say, 1946 to 1950—
must now seem to Americans under the age of forty almost as distant in time as the Sphinx and the pyramids of ancient Egypt. But
the career of George F. Kennan narrows the years. People of my
generation know him as the distinguished American diplomat who,
as deputy chief of mission at the U. S. embassy in Moscow, sent
the so-called "long telegram" to Washington one day in 1946. That
famous dispatch quickly assumed the status of a state paper, brilliantly analyzing the "sources of Soviet conduct," and was ultimately published under that title in the journal *Foreign Affairs*.
Kennan, as a serving diplomat, thought it unseemly to associate his
name with it. He signed it "Mr. X," and thereafter it was known to
all as the "Mr. X article."

Kennan brought a great fund of observation, study and firsthand
experience to Russian affairs. He had been with the first U. S. delegation to enter Moscow after Franklin D. Roosevelt restored diplomatic relations with Bolshevik Russia in 1933. Russian language,

literature, culture and politics were his professional passion. Thus it was that when the Big Three wartime alliance began to fray in 1946, Kennan was uniquely positioned to help Americans understand the sources of tension and to chart an official response to the new Soviet hostility. The Mr. X article outlined a strategy which soon became known as "containment." It argued that the most valuable weapons available to this country were the force of democratic example and the values of the open society. These, he said, should be firmly exploited while Soviet aggression was firmly resisted. In time, he predicted, Stalinism would falter and an internal mellowing process would set in. As director of the State Department's Policy Planning Council under President Truman, Kennan helped fashion a foreign policy embodying the containment idea, although he resisted what he frequently described as its "militarization."

After retiring from the Foreign Service and spending most of the 1950s as an independent scholar and writer, Kennan returned briefly to diplomatic service as President Kennedy's ambassador to Yugoslavia. But his forte seemed almost from the first to be that of a detached observer. And even if his contribution to postwar strategy had been less notable, his distinction as a writer of history would be secure. His books on early U. S.-Soviet relations, *Russia Leaves the War* and *The Decision to Intervene*, won well-deserved prizes. His two-volume memoir is a literary classic. His trilogy on the origins of World War I (of which two volumes have appeared, *The Decline of Bismarck's European Order* and *The Strange Alliance*) are likewise enthralling works of the highest historical merit.

Mr. Kennan has continued all along to be oddly controversial. I was present at the Washington headquarters of the Council on Foreign Relations on the evening in February 1977 when he reviewed the containment doctrine in a talk immediately seized upon by his detractors—and even by some admirers—as fighting words. Mr. Kennan seemed almost to have lost faith, as he had lost patience, with his earlier counsels. He described the Mr. X article as one that "has dogged my footsteps . . . like a faithful but unwanted and somewhat embarrassing little animal." Now, he proposed a plan for retrieving a lost national consensus regarding the nature and purposes of the Soviet leadership.

It was not my first encounter with the prophet of containment. Twenty years earlier, I had been a student at Oxford when Kennan came there in 1957–58 as George Eastman professor. He was a great success, as he always is at whatever engages his interest, and repeatedly filled a large hall at the schools in the High Street with an audience of students and dons spellbound by the vivid lectures later published as *Russia and the West Under Lenin and Stalin.*

One gray October day, not long after he arrived, some of us invited him to lunch in a back room at the King's Arms pub. Among those present were a number who later distinguished themselves in public life, academia and journalism, including Rocky Suddarth, later U. S. ambassador to Jordan; Neil Rudenstine, the president of Harvard University; and Willie Morris, editor of *Harper's Magazine* in the late 1960s and 1970s, a journalist and memoirist of distinction. On that occasion some of us noticed for the first time a striking contradiction—or what seemed so—in Mr. Kennan. The historian whose writings and lectures displayed so firm a grasp of the irrationalities and passions of revolutionaries, and the illusions of democratic idealists, was an incurable rationalist when it came to American politics. He argued to us that what was really needed in the U. S. was a "disinterested" third party of public-spirited critics whose good faith would be attested to by their resolute avoidance of office or power. It was a favorite theme of his at the time. It was the virginal innocence of his ideas about internal democratic politics that provoked Isaiah Berlin's quip that Mr. Kennan believed in government "by a nest of brooding Salazars."

Now, here he was in Washington twenty years later, attempting once again to chart a program of political action whose similarities to the disinterested party of critics were striking. When word of his remarks began to circulate in Washington, they were harshly criticized. The most caustic of his critics, and in many ways the most unlikely, was the late Henry Fairlie, successively Washington correspondent of the *Times* of London and contributing editor of *The New Republic*. In *The New Republic* of December 24, under the heading "Mr. X Squared," Fairlie dismissed Kennan's talk at the

Council on Foreign Relations as an arrogant exercise in "the politics of senility," the effort of "an old man of the establishment" to make up for old misjudgments and to rehabilitate a discredited "elite consensus" on Russian policy. Fairlie, however, had not been present at the talk and missed the spirit of the occasion.

Here, as I reconstruct it, was the essence of what Kennan said: Stalin's death, the restoration of Western Europe to health and confidence, the complexity of the strategic arms race, and the collapse of the illusory unity in the world Communist movement—all these factors had utterly altered the world and the balance of power since the appearance of his Mr. X article, and not to our disadvantage. Kennan, always hostile to nuclear weaponry, confessed his bewilderment by "the fantastic reaches of . . . military mathematics—the mathematics of mutual destruction in an age of burgeoning weapons technology." In such technology he found "a distinct unreality," and he thought it essential to move the military rivalry off center stage and concentrate on "the nature of the Soviet leadership and . . . the discipline exerted upon it by its own experience, problems, and political necessities." It was, he said, the clashing and discordant American views about the nature and purposes of the Soviet leaders—then, as earlier—that accounted for the drift and lack of focus in American policy, which, he went on to say, had been "lamed" by that discord.

It is fair to say that Mr. Kennan's audience that evening in 1977, while respectful, was skeptical, though not for the reasons Fairlie and others assumed—not because Kennan waved away "military mathematics" or because he considered thoughtful opposition to detente or arms control misinformed, though he did, but because he seemed, characteristically, to minimize the "emotional" barriers to productive strategic thinking. Not everyone agreed with Mr. Kennan that "the problem is, after all, a cognitive one," or shared his unyielding rationalist optimism that, after examining together "a given body of factual material," persons of good will would assent to its validity.

Here again, it seemed to me that evening, was the engaging paradox of the great scholar-diplomat: he is impatient with, almost physically pained by, domestic political conflict and tends to believe that it is rooted in ignorance or misunderstanding rather than in clashes of temperament, interests and values. No one, unless it was Kennan's historical master Edward Gibbon, has written of great events with a surer grasp of the elements of caprice, passion, vanity, folly and temper in the events of the past. And yet—this is the paradox—no one entertains loftier hopes of human reason in the present. There almost seem to be two Kennans. If you have read the historian Kennan on the flounderings of American policy in the face of the Russian revolution, or the obtuseness with which those pariahs of the 1920s, Soviet Russia and Weimar Germany, were treated by the victorious Western powers, or the oddities leading to the pronouncement of the U. S. Open Door policy vis-a-vis the old China—if you have read these and other episodes of Kennanite history, you come away with a sense of the irrationalities and ironies that shape historical events. But if you read his earnest and sober appeals to reason in various policy papers and journalistic pieces, you encounter a policymaker who seems to ignore the very elements of folly and vanity he evokes so tellingly as a historian.

One can only speculate on this apparent contradiction. Mr. Kennan is that strange and rare species, the truly dispassionate and disinterested observer, and he supposes others to be likewise. One whose outlook has been so tempered and chastened by his own investigations of the past has difficulty understanding why we in the present fail to heed its clear lessons. In that sense, Kennan the historian is the adversary of Kennan the policymaker, the one a pessimist and the other an optimist about our capacity for dealing clearly—"cognitively," as he might say—with current strategic problems. One thing he certainly is not, however, is "an old man of the establishment," as Fairlie charged, seeking to compensate for past errors or organizing conspiratorial seminars in "the politics of senility." This harsh language does no justice to the Kennan who wears no one's collar and who is intellectually tentative and modest to a fault. Near the end of his talk in November 1977, he said: "I am much aware that it is exactly fifty years ago this year that I entered on my own career as a so-called Russian expert, and . . . it is time that my ideas, too, were taken thoroughly apart and put together again with relation, this time, to the present scene and not to all the memories I cherish."

He was, as usual, too hard on himself and his earlier ideas. The outcome of the cold war and the encouraging revolution of the 1990s in Russia and Eastern Europe have demonstrated again, if further proof were needed, that the Mr. X of 1946–47 knew very well what he was talking about.

Skeletons in the
National Closet

EVERY NATION CELEBRATES its better historical moments. A sterner test of national character is how nations deal with their mistakes and embarrassments, the skeletons in the closet of history.

Like the Ministry of Truth in George Orwell's novel *Nineteen Eighty-four*, police states dispatch bad memories down the "memory hole," making inconvenient facts into nonfacts. They also invent bogus facts, as when the czarist secret police forged the so-called Protocols of the Elders of Zion, a document that has served as one of the foundations of twentieth-century anti-Semitism.

In their better moments, by contrast, free societies confess error. A notable example was the official recognition, in 1988, of the injustices the United States did to citizens of Japanese ancestry who were interned after the attack on Pearl Harbor in January 1941. As national memories go, the panic that followed Pearl Harbor and its cost to a highly visible and vulnerable group of American citizens is neither proud nor pleasant.

After Pearl Harbor, a Japanese attack on the West Coast was

thought to be possible, and Japanese Americans were suspected, baselessly, of being spies, or "fifth columnists," a sinister term for the internally disloyal that had been coined during the recent Spanish civil war. The West Coast was designated a war zone, subject to military rule, and some 112,000 Japanese Americans, native citizens as well as the naturalized and aliens, were shipped to "relocation centers" in the American interior.

The injustice of this proceeding is now almost universally conceded. Congress voted modest property compensation years ago, but the offense to the loyalty of the internees and their families was not officially acknowledged until Congress passed legislation in 1988 tendering formal apologies in the nation's behalf. For reasons never made entirely clear, the Justice Department opposed the legislation, viewing it as a gratuitous exercise in hindsight, insulting to the authorities of 1942, although it more nearly resembled the acts of oblivion that followed some European civil wars. Such acts make no attempt to settle scores that are beyond settlement; that is just the point. They acknowledge that blame and recrimination are not useful categories when a bitter issue has been resolved—that, while we can't dodge accountability for the past, we can dispense with vengeance.

Even with the Reagan administration in opposition, the bill easily cleared both houses of Congress. But the response of a small band of determined opponents in the Senate showed how easily an obvious point can be missed. Sen. Jesse Helms of North Carolina oafishly equated the Japanese Americans to whom the apology was extended with the Japanese civil and military officials who planned and carried out the bombing of Pearl Harbor—or their descendents. "Fair is fair," the senator said, offering an amendment to "provide that no funds shall be appropriated under this title until the government of Japan has fairly compensated the families of the men and women who were killed as a result of the . . . bombing of Pearl Harbor."

The elusive "fairness" of this bizarre proposal was obscured by its stark irony. After Pearl Harbor, certain law-abiding U. S. citizens were summarily stripped of their rights, property, and, in the case of some elderly people, life itself, and shipped off to drafty quonset huts on the plains. Unlike Americans of German or Italian descent, distantly related to citizens of the other nations with which we were at war, Japanese Americans had the bad luck to be racially identifiable, and they paid a hideous price. Senator Helms's weird notion of fair play was that they once again be held hostage for the same remote racial connection to the Japanese in Japan that cost them so heavily in the first place, even though they are as American as the senator—perhaps more so, in their grasp of what the Constitution is all about.

Americans have moved a step or two closer since 1942 to understanding the mischief of policies based on racial stereotypes and distinctions. Japanese Americans were exposed to prejudiced treatment, lawless in spirit and unwarranted in fact. The only significant West Coast spy ring had been centered in the Los Angeles consulate of the imperial Japanese government, but naval intelligence and the FBI had cracked that cell months before Pearl Harbor. While the navy and the FBI cautioned against hasty action, the removal and internment proceeded. President Roosevelt ordered it, the army carried it out and Congress endorsed it with hasty legislation. Institutions usually relied upon to have second thoughts—even the American Civil Liberties Union and the Supreme Court—trailed along. Walter Lippmann, the most eminent newspaper pundit of his day, approved. Earl Warren, later chief justice and a great civil libertarian, backed the internment as attorney general of California. Justice Hugo Black, normally a dependable critic of arbitrary invasions of personal liberty, voted in three Supreme Court cases to uphold the internment policy. The only notable dissenter was Sen. Robert A. Taft, hero of the Republican conservatives, who questioned the enabling legislation as the Senate was casually whooping it through.

It is significant that no parallel hysteria broke out in Hawaii, where the immediate victims of Pearl Harbor lived, presumably because people of Japanese ancestry were not a vulnerable minority in the islands, and racial prejudice has never been as virulent there as on the mainland. But aside from slavery and various sharp practices upon the Indian tribes (and slaves and Indians were long deemed not to be citizens), the internment of the Japanese Americans is the worst blot of its sort on our history.

What Congress attempted to do by way of balancing the ledgers in 1988 seems to me to make a fundamental point about historical responsibility. Along with what Jefferson called "the blessings of liberty," Americans inherit the burden of the past as well: a legacy of misdeeds and injustices. That legacy raises no issue of "hereditary" or collective guilt. Yet the integrity of a nation professing a belief in historical justice depends upon the free acknowledgment of errors, for much the same reason that confession is said to be good for the soul.

GAMES
HISTORIANS
PLAY

❧

Docudrama, Film and the Limits of Fabrication

WITH THE ADVENT of the new (and rather self-contradictory) form of entertainment known as "docudrama," the borders between history and fabrication are more actively contested than ever. Many Americans now apparently gather their notions of what happened in the past directly from movies and television, and indistinct lines are drawn between truth, conjecture and outright fabrication. There are advanced thinkers, self-described "postmodernists," who profess to be untroubled by this. They take the view that because history is necessarily a reconstruction, and often a very subjective one, its inevitable "indeterminacy" has at last rid us of the impression that *any* history is reliable. Therefore, they say, we might as well construct it to suit our fancy, fact and fiction being equally invented, or as they like to say "parabolic."

Certainly the postmodern view of history gets a constant work-out in the American movie industry, with mixed results that range from dismal to inspiring.

Consider Spike Lee's film *Malcolm X*, for instance. The movie was eagerly embraced as spiritual revelation by millions of young black men and women when it appeared in 1994, even though much of it involves demonstrable fable and fabrication, drawn from *The Autobiography of Malcolm X* ghosted by the late Alex Haley of *Roots* fame. Years after re-creating Malcolm X, Haley, ironically, was caught out in a substantial fictionalization of his own commercially successful story of slave ancestry. Such fabrications may now be too solidly entrenched, and too useful in the creation of heroic mythology, to be easily countered. But every viewer of Lee's movie ought at least to be aware of them.

In principle, none of this is exactly new. Shakespeare has been criticized through the years for doctoring the record in his history plays—especially in the notorious case of Richard III. His sources were themselves questionable in some cases, and, indeed, the sort of "history" Holinshed and others wrote bore interesting resemblance to the exemplary and heroic idealizations that pass now for fact in "docudrama." There was also, of course, the famous case of Mason Weems's early iconic biography of George Washington with its wholesome and charming fables about the first president's boyhood. The same may be said of much of the postassassination treatment of Lincoln, beginning with William Herndon's life. The form may now be electronic; the practice remains in some ways as it has been for centuries.

Those who worry on gloomy days that postmodern influence in history is doing strange things to our respect for the past will find cold comfort in a revealing *New York Times Magazine* piece about E. L. Doctorow, the clever author of *Ragtime* and other best-selling novels. Doctorow is noted for the creation of pseudohistorical scenes and ambiences, often so realistic as to be indistinguishable from historical fact. In *Ragtime,* for instance, Doctorow not only includes a good bit of fairly reliable social documentation but also impishly introduces a scene in which the tycoons Henry Ford and J. P. Morgan meet in a secret nocturnal rendezvous to discuss Rosicrucianism. The picture is so deftly drawn that it reads like history, but it is fantasy.

Taking minor and amusing liberties with history can be harmless, but the popularity of "docudrama" and the readiness of young audiences to swallow it indiscriminately bring into prospect a time when most of us won't know history from hokum. Every organized society requires (or at least has so far required) some sort of accepted historical foundation. If it can't be found in the record, a pseudopast will usually be substituted. From John Locke to Karl Marx, influential political theorists have contrived an imaginary history; those who lack the art to compare it with what may actually be documented are liable to be seduced by it, sometimes with unpleasant consequences. Doctorow dismisses such concerns. "I think fiction intrudes on history," he told the *New York Times*. "It always has . . . the whole idea of objective historical reality is naive. . . . Historians know they're not objective. Why should fiction writers be denied the composition of history?"

That confusing mouthful glides, with typical postmodernist ease, over a number of basic distinctions. A literal idea of "historical reality," history free of the observer's biases, may indeed be naive, but there is a radical difference between a documentable past, however playfully examined, and outright fabrication. Suppose, for instance, that a chief justice of the U.S. Supreme Court should invoke an American past in which even free-born black people (never mind slaves) had been considered "so far inferior" to white people as to enjoy no rights of citizenship at all. Today, such an assertion would be greeted with outrage, and historians would rise up on every hand to refute it. But that is exactly how Chief Justice Taney justified the Dred Scott decision in 1857, when he ruled that a former slave had no standing to sue in the federal courts to vindicate his freedom. Or suppose, to bring the story forward a jump or two, that a president explained his view of the role of federal judges by doctoring the plain truth about the Constitution. Ronald Reagan, explaining why he would not appoint "judicial activists," said that they might annul decisions made at the ballot box. According to Reagan, the framers of the Constitution "placed the appointive power in the hands of those who are in office as a result of popular election." But he did not mention that the framers deliberately distanced exercise of executive power, including the appointment of judges, from elections. Judges were originally to be nominated by a president picked by an electoral college of notables and confirmed by a body whose members, in turn, were elected by state legislatures. Reagan's insinuation that judges were intended to be closely attuned to the outcome of "popular elections" was simply a fiction, well off the mark historically. The Jefferson administration tried during the third president's first term to establish that judges could be politically removed by impeachment. But the effort fell flat when impeachment charges against Justice Samuel Chase failed. It may be less naive than E. L. Doctorow thinks to believe in "historical reality." Novelists will dicker with the past, as is their privilege. But playfulness of the *Ragtime* variety is a long way from cooking history for dangerous purposes.

Given the obvious dangers, however, the critics of docudrama occasionally find their theoretical objections embarrassed by highly successful films or novels that work. How, for instance, does one justify an indecent enthusiasm for a movie that took gross liberties with Mozart's life and death, and even grosser ones with the character of his supposed rival Salieri?

Perhaps, as the old Latin adage has it, *Quod licet Jovi non licet bovi*: What is permitted to Jove is denied to a dumb ox. *Amadeus* is so lordly a prank with history as to render its distortions almost irrelevant. I am sure that neither the scriptwriter, Peter Shaffer, nor the director, Milos Forman, wasted their tears over issues of veracity, any more than Shakespeare did when he dramatized the Richard III he found in the pages of Holinshed's *Chronicles*. Drama often selects and molds its raw materials with shameless arbitrariness, having an eye to epitome rather than literalism. Its aim is to play variations on universal themes, and the theme of *Amadeus* is the absoluteness of art, and music, the most absolute of the arts, at that.

By portraying Mozart as a foul-mouthed, lecherous, lusty and endearing eighteenth-century punk, and his rival Salieri as a prig, *Amadeus* makes a paradoxical point. The highest art often springs, like roses from dunghills, from improbable composts and is its own justification. For years after Mozart's early death, rumors buzzed about Vienna that Salieri, court composer to Emperor Joseph II, had poisoned him. Shaffer didn't invent the story or use it first. Pushkin, and later Rimsky-Korsakov, mined the same tale.

In Shaffer's retelling, Salieri is a journeyman professional musician who, in a twist on the Faust legend, bargains his soul in return for musical inspiration. He promises to be a good boy—as the world estimates good boys—if only God will make him a chosen instrument. God grants the wish, up to a point—the point that separates professional competence from genius. Encountering the impish genius Mozart, Salieri is dismayed by God's fickleness and favoritism. And, indeed, for conventional moralists, the dunghill/ rose connection is always a painful reminder that man's ways and whims aren't necessarily in accord with divine purposes. Having faced that hard truth, *Amadeus* also faces another, comparatively minor but dramatically useful: that great art usually flouts academic convention. In *Amadeus*, received musical opinion is amusingly embodied in the amiable fuddy-duddies who advise the emperor on what is suitable. These arbiters of taste are shown giving the inventive Mozart no end of grief over such trifling issues as the "morality" of setting an opera in a whorehouse, or of mixing ballet and opera in the same form, or of composing a libretto in German rather than Italian.

Whether or not any such tyranny of musical convention thwarted Mozart, it is as central to the theme of art's absolute license as is Salieri's soured bargain with God. Academic rigidity is shown driving Mozart to resort to folk opera, to "vulgar" audiences, as the background for his imperishable *Magic Flute*. *Amadeus* is a brilliant yarn, a powerful fable, compounded of half-truth, harmless invention and historical nonsense. But the fictitious Salieri may live longer than the historical one.

As nearly as old medical puzzles may be solved through inference from slight evidence, it has been speculated that Mozart died of Bright's disease, a kidney disorder, not by poison—and certainly not of weariness or fright induced by Salieri dressed as the ghost of his demanding father and scolding him about his unfinished Requiem. *Amadeus* pretends to be nothing other than what it is, an exalted tale woven from historical scraps that makes enduring points about God, man and music, and makes them so well that its

risk their lives in struggles whose significance is elusive in the microcosms of battle. Still more remarkably, warriors—at least those who honor the ancient chivalric codes, as most soliders on both sides did during our Civil War—accept the constraint of laws and customs that combine deadliness with good manners and even with a touch of brotherly feeling for the foe. That was still the case when the Army of the Potomac met Robert E. Lee's Army of Northern Virginia in late June 1863 at a Pennsylvania hamlet where ten roads met. It was the epitome of the Civil War and perhaps its decisive encounter.

The movie is based on Michael Shaara's fine novel *The Killer Angels,* a gem that the readers of *American Heritage* magazine recently ranked, with justice, among the crowning works of historical fiction. Shaara's strategy for penetrating the fog of war was to focus on major historical characters—not only Lee and his main corps commander, James Longstreet, but the valiant Col. Lawrence Chamberlain of Maine, a sometime Bowdoin College professor of rhetoric and religion who won the Medal of Honor conducting his unit's defense of Little Round Top on the second day. Little Round Top was the southern anchor of the Union line, the horseshoe nail the loss of which the battle itself and the kingdom might have been lost.

The Killer Angels and the movie *Gettysburg* offer a useful lesson which dealers in historical junk never seem to learn. Both are, so far as I can tell, scrupulously factual. Both also reach beyond what is known to imagine what might have been done or said, fictionalizing without falsifying. It is a crucial distinction. Longstreet, Lee's right arm after the death of Stonewall Jackson at Chancellorsville in May of the year before, had absorbed the grim lesson of entrenched defensive positions in the age of riflery and cannister. It was a lesson that still eluded stupid commanders on the Western front of World War I half a century later. At Gettysburg, foreseeing the dreadful outcome of marching up a long slope in the face of well-defended fire, Longstreet was too choked with foreboding to give the verbal order for Pickett's charge. That advance up Cemetery Ridge on the third day of the great battle defied the lesson that should have been learned from the frightening Union casualties at Fredericksburg in the previous December and dealt the South a setback from which it never recovered. That is historical fact, well documented.

On the other hand, we can only imagine what Lee said privately to his skylarking young cavalry commander, Jeb Stuart, when Stuart returned from gallivanting about the countryside. He had left Lee's army "blinded"—i. e., without reliable intelligence of the enemy's whereabouts—for the better part of a week. We also know the legend of Longstreet's supposed sulky "delay" in deploying his corps on the second day, but it is legend only, a canard concocted by Longstreet's political enemies years after the war when Longstreet became a Republican and a supporter of national reconciliation. We can guess Longstreet's inward agony as he contemplates Lee's battle plan. In giving voice and action to these teasing but critical historical silences, fiction has a role, when it is as well written as Schaara's. The director of the movie, Ronald Maxwell, became obsessed with Schaara's novel when it appeared almost a quarter century ago. The movie offers fine portraits of some of the key figures, though no student of Robert E. Lee can quite believe in the mincing figure Martin Sheen makes of him. Sheen's Virginia accent sounds like a Hollywood actor of the second rank trying to talk like a Virginian. *Gettysburg* hardly solves the mystery of war, but good war stories are about self-transcendance. War depends on the strange but essential conviction that some causes are preferable to life itself. What Ken Burns began to do with his magnificent public broadcasting series on the Civil War, the makers of *Gettysburg* creditably continued.

The same can hardly said of Oliver Stone, who with his wacky movie on the Kennedy assassination, *JFK*, emerged as a major counterfeiter of historical truth. During a classroom discussion of the movie at Washington and Lee, I asked thirty-five bright sophomores a question: Suppose you distrust Stone's version of the assassination (they obviously did). How would you check your doubts against what can be known? Startlingly, not one proposed recourse to written records, those in the Warren Commission's twenty-six supplementary volumes or elsewhere. They suggested that perhaps there must be other films or television programs that take the view that Kennedy's assassin acted alone, and that these could be checked against Oliver Stone's. We live in an age in which, for the young, electronically generated moods, impressions and images often carry at least as much weight as cold print, which indeed has never been colder to the touch.

The proliferation of skeptical books about the Warren Commission and its theory that Lee Harvey Oswald acted alone—now almost of library strength—suggests an intractable public suspicion that the truth has yet to be told about Kennedy's death, and Stone exploits that suspicion. The irony is that the conspiracy theorists thrive not on a paucity of evidence but on a bewildering abundance of circumstantial detail. But fact alone cannot be the problem here.

Rather, the problem is a new conception of historicity, its limits and requirements. To the extent that standard investigative techniques, or rules of evidence that every courtroom reporter becomes acquainted with, have ever been widely understood, they are wasting assets today. That explains in part why Stone's fantasies, and his exaltation of figures like the late New Orleans district attorney Jim Garrison, can be thought to outweigh the sober, systematic documentation assembled by the Warren Commission.

The more I reflect on the intractability of the conspiracy theories of Kennedy's murder, the more I am drawn to William Manchester's theory. Manchester, the journalist and historian initially commissioned by the Kennedy family to write his gigantic account, *The Death of a President*, suggests that we resist the idea that, in history, huge effects may flow from slight causes. The troubled, neurotic and historically microscopic Lee Harvey Oswald was nothing if not a slight cause. Gerald Posner's book *Case Closed,* a persuasive reexamination of the case, dwells upon the triviality of Oswald as a shaper of history. He was a hapless misfit, unemployable, loveless, semiliterate, incompetent, with fantasies of heroic fame and fortune. How could this young man, armed with a cheap mail-order surplus rifle, have made so catastrophic a dent in American history and in our national self-regard? As well might one ask, as Hannah Arendt did in her book on the trial of Adolf Eichmann, how the murder of millions could be engineered by a bland German bureaucrat. She called it "the banality of evil," and it is an eternal constant

of the human story. Few Macbeths or Richard IIIs, few large villains, find their way beyond the pages of ancient chronicle and
drama into the news. Like the miserable Eichmann, Oswald fell far
short of evil on the grand scale. He was closer to a zero, reminding
us of the ancient mythic connection of evil with nothingness, with
naught (hence the word "naughty," now purged of all its old force).
Yet Oswald fits the usual profile of those twisted loners who con-
tribute so handsomely to the sum of human unhappiness.

It has been speculated, apparently on the basis of some suspicions
of which Lyndon Johnson spoke not long before his death, that the
fear of provoking another dangerous nuclear confrontation could
have prompted senior officials to stifle their hunch about the so-
called Cuban connection—arising from Oswald's known visit to the
Cuban and Soviet consulates in Mexico City a few weeks before the
assassination. But the fact is among the strongest indications that
he was not part of a conspiracy. He sought a visa to go to Cuba,
and had he obtained what he sought, he couldn't have been in Dallas on November 22, 1963.

Yet the "nuclear danger" theory is a more generous speculation
about official behavior than that offered by Stone, whose film *JFK*
updates the "merchants of death" legend of the 1930s. Credulous
believers in that disarming historical myth persuaded themselves
that the United States had been lured against its will into World
War I in 1917 by munitions makers and holders of Allied bonds
and their collaborators and agents. Stone now intimates that a
shadowy "military-industrial complex" (not by a wide mark the
brazen money-making machine warned of in Dwight D. Eisenhower's farewell address) feared that Kennedy would withdraw from
Vietnam and that Pentagon order books would shrink. He had to
be bumped off to keep the war going. But when Stone's supposed
conspirators were spinning their elaborate web, America's investment of men and equipment in Vietnam was much too slight to
have mattered either way.

As of the making of his sequel movie, *Nixon*, Oliver Stone was
still hawking shadowy and sinister conspiracies. But one could at
least detect just an inkling of a sense of humor in *Nixon*, inasmuch
as the center of the great conspiracy now seems to be J. R. Ewing,

the brazen manipulator of the Friday evening soap opera *Dallas*, played brilliantly in a cameo role by Larry Hagman.

One writer has observed that the Warren Commission report has "grave deficiencies as history," a proposition with which all can readily agree, whatever their view of Stone's version. If by deficiency one means that the Warren Commission committed its share of omissions and oversights, inevitable in any complex investigative enterprise, the point is incontestable. So long as revisionism is possible, the received version of history, official or scholarly, is never unshakeable; it is simply the most plausible and disciplined theory of a set of random facts.

And that leads to a larger, and concluding, point about historicity. History is often thought of as a fixed and impregnable version of the past, imperishable and immutable. But history, properly understood, is an "inquiry" (the root meaning of the word), and, in that sense, history is always "deficient" or, to use a more accurate term, provisional. It involves a human effort to make sequential sense of an imperfect record, in this and every tale of high crime and misfortune. The investigator of any historical mystery, like a prosecutor forming a hypothesis about a complex criminal case, must shape a "story" from events that were not storylike to begin with, that may have exhibited no clear internal logic as they unfolded. If such events could speak, they would protest that they had no idea, as they occurred, that they constituted any sort of "story." But that all stories can only be human constructs out of near-chaos need not invalidate them.

Notwithstanding this familiar limitation of historical inquiry, almost every conspiracy theory of the Kennedy assassination reveals an exalted expectation which, in the nature of things, can't be satisfied. In the world of conspiracists, there are no blunders or accidents, no unintended consequences, no mere coincidence or happenstance. The world is an orderly and planned place. It could be said of conspiracists, as the late John P. Roche once wrote, that "one of the problems in politics, as in life generally, is that analysts get too subtle. The classic example . . . occurred at the Congress of Vienna in 1815 when Prince Metternich, learning that the Russian ambassador had suddenly died, asked, 'What could have been his motive?' "

Conspiracy theories, being similarly over-ingenious, are missing those features that constantly muddle the everyday world we live in—whether the blunders of bureaucrats or FBI directors fearing that uncontrolled revelations might compromise four decades of carefully cultivated myth. (The FBI had long had its eye on Oswald, but lost track of him in Dallas, and J. Edgar Hoover wasn't eager that this embarrassing fact be widely known.) In the conspiracists' world, people are credulous about the doubtful and doubtful about the obvious.

That is why the Kennedy murder mystery will never be solved to their satisfaction. It can't be, by rules that assume that history can establish unimpeachable certainty. The solution that skeptics seek must be the exception to the rule that history is always provisional, always "deficient" in its vulnerability to disturbance by new information or better theory. The real question about the Kennedy assassination is whether any critic—especially Oliver Stone—has disturbed, let alone overturned, the Warren Commission's verdict. The answer so far is no.

As all the foregoing reflections surely reveal, no one—certainly not the present writer—can afford to take an inflexible view of film or television docudrama—not one, at any rate, that is immune to being stretched out of shape by individual cases like *Amadeus* or *Mississippi Burning*, whose dramatic merit excuses their liberties with the historical record. Poetic license and dramatic necessity have their claims. But fictionalization for valid dramatic purposes, when it is clearly identified as such, is easily distinguished from the fabrications practiced in a film like *JFK*. Those who casually indulge in fabrications should understand that there is little to distinguish them, ethically, from the infamous and sinister fabrications of the past. Perhaps the most notorious of all was the "Protocols of the Learned Elders of Zion," an incendiary document, now believed to have been forged in old czarist Russia by the secret police. It has been one of the foundation stones of twentieth-century anti-Semitism. That deadly example alone should suffice to warn that when we make exceptions to the spirit of historical truth, we should make certain that the purpose is to instruct and amuse, not to degrade, deceive and injure.

Barbara Tuchman and the
Horseshoe Nails of History

WHEN BARBARA TUCHMAN died in February 1989, leaving behind a long shelf of readable historical best-sellers, the *New York
Times* remarked in an editorial tribute that "stuffy professorial reviews" of her work hadn't mattered because she had "made readers
care about a thousand dusty yesterdays." The premise that readabil-
ity and accuracy or depth need be at odds in historical writing is a
familiar but mischievous notion, fostered by parties on both sides
of the imagined barrier.

Barbara Tuchman would have done well to take the professorial
reviewers more seriously than she did. But the gulf between the
gifted amateur and the professional student of history is a relatively
recent, and often pointless, problem in American culture. It
emerged only as historical study and writing began to be profes-
sionalized a century ago. Most of the early master historians writing
in English, here and in England (Parkman, Prescott, Adams, Macaulay and Gibbon, to mention five) were self-schooled amateurs.
The closest among the five to a historical professional was Henry

Adams, the writer of the great *History of the United States During the Administrations of Thomas Jefferson and James Madison*, who had studied in Germany and for years conducted one of the earliest university historical seminars at Harvard.

Barbara Tuchman, their successor in the school of amateur history, was of undoubted importance. In both intellect and style, she towered over most historical popularizers—and for that matter over most of her detractors within the academy. Her books engaged lay readers because they epitomized the old idea that history should be a vivid act of storytelling in which cause and effect emerge unobscured by pedantic hemming and hawing. She always took a strong dramatic line. In her most celebrated book, *The Guns of August*, she related how a calamitous world war began in August 1914 in a random train of events that had been neither planned nor willed by those who found themselves sliding into the conflict. Her ability to establish a vivid narrative line was what newspaper salutes cited as exceptional at the time of her death, and it was almost invariably said that her storytelling talent separated her from dry-as-dust professors. Sneering at scholars is, of course, an occupational vice of journalism, and the sneers are often reciprocated.

But even as Barbara Tuchman achieved her remarkable ascendancy, the unfruitful divergence between amateurs and professionals in the writing of history continued to widen. Glib popularizers, even fictionalizers, won acclaim with the new bastard form, sometimes called "docudrama," while scholarly historical specialists, with their ever narrowing focus, forfeited popular audiences. It would be agreeable, and rather gallant, to say that because Barbara Tuchman wrote enchanting historical narrative, the depth and accuracy of her judgments didn't matter—the point apparently intended by the *New York Times* editorialist. But that would be an insult to her memory, for she was serious indeed about history. Her flair for storytelling and drama prompted her on more than one occasion to simplify historical causation. In her books, great matters are constantly seen as pivoting on small provocations: The British lost an empire in North America because of the "folly" of a numbskull eighteenth-century aristocracy, frivolous about serious political duties. Or Turkey entered the First World War on the side of the central powers for no other reason than that a German battle cruiser, eluding the Royal Navy, took shelter in Constantinople. Or the famous Zimmerman telegram, in which the German foreign office solicited Mexico's intervention in World War I by dangling before our Latin neighbor the prospect of recovering her "lost provinces," craftily exploited by British intelligence, explained American intervention in 1917. All this made for vividness and excitement, but it also catered to simplistic conceptions of historical cause and effect that good historians ought to steer us away from.

It is true that Tuchman's professorial detractors often seemed to go to opposite extremes. They became frightened of significant conclusions about the past, wandering in the voguish wastelands of quantification. Or, following the French annalist school, they reduced history to an anthropological inquiry into the baking of bread, religion, dancing, or burial customs in some obscure corner of the past. Had Barbara Tuchman chosen to devote more of her energy and intelligence to a more serious consideration of historiographical issues, for which she entertained a certain puzzled contempt, she might have bridged the two worlds to the improvement of both.

Say what one will of her failings, however, a new book by Barbara Tuchman was always a delight to read, overflowing with vivid "lessons," however disconcerting they might be to those who tend to find historical causation a bit trickier than she did. One of her last books, *The March of Folly* (1984), exemplified her strengths and weaknesses.

She took as her theme "the pursuit of policy against self-interest," a form of folly abundant in history and, Tuchman observed, "ubiquitous" in our time. The idea for the book almost certainly sprang from the author's distaste for the war in Vietnam, seasoned with a few reflections on parallel instances of folly in the past. For illustration, she examined three episodes in addition to Vietnam, one mythic and two historical. The mythic episode was the story of the Trojan horse. The two historical examples were the misbehavior of six Renaissance popes, which in her view "provoked" the Protestant Reformation, and Britain's loss of her North American colonies.

The rather anomalous curtain-raiser in *The March of Folly* is the story of the Trojan horse, presented as the prototype of historical folly. The tale may have had actual antecedents, but so far as we know it is pure invention—which is to say that its calamitous effect for the Trojans was ordained by the poets who imagined it, retrieved it from oral tradition and folk tale or embellished it in song and rhyme: Homer in *The Odyssey* and Virgil in the second book of the *Aeneid*. The story may be a suggestive prototype of historical folly, but for fairly obvious reasons its value as history is nil. History proper—at least the kind of history that is supposed to teach us lessons—demands alternatives; it demands the exercise of free will and free choice. We must see that the outcome might have been otherwise than it was. But the Trojans who ignored the warnings of Laocoon and Cassandra, admitting the fateful gift horse to their city, were fated by a caucus of the gods to do so. Cassandra's prophecies were destined to be disbelieved; that was her curse. The Trojans had no real choice. Their "folly" was arranged beforehand on Mount Olympus.

So far as we know, the other historical follies Tuchman conjoined to the tale of the Trojan horse were not contrived by the gods on Mount Olympus to satisfy supernatural vanities or enmities. But each was different, and each raises a different kind of historical question.

Doubtless, the gross malfeasance of the six worldly popes from Sixtus IV to Clement VII reflected little credit on their great office. "To each," Tuchman writes, "Saint Peter's see was the supreme pork barrel." Their crass and gaudy incumbencies lowered the papacy in popular regard. But did the misfeasance of these popes really "provoke" the Protestant secession? Tuchman does not persuasively establish the connection; too many links are missing. For instance, the pivotal figure of Martin Luther gets a page or two, while Calvin and other central reformers go entirely unmentioned. A historical view of the Protestant secession would have to take far ampler note of Luther and of larger and more various influences than papal pranks. One suspects that even if the likes of Leo X and Julius II had been meek and monkish men, the impact of print and of rising nationalism, of the worldly spirit of art and inquiry, would have set up powerful centrifugal forces within the church universal.

Tuchman's vivid treatment of the loss of Britain's North American empire is likewise flawed by narrow focus. It is fun to read or write about the insouciance and extravagance of the eighteenth-century English aristocracy, and their follies certainly contributed to the loss of the American colonies. She justly accuses the English statesmen of the age—including King George III—of knowing too little about the American colonies, of dogmatism, of various forms of impulsiveness and "wooden-headedness" (one of Tuchman's favorite terms of abuse). She makes an exception only of the decrepit Lord Chatham, writing, in a typical assignment of great effects to a single cause, that "if Chatham had been healthy the history of America would have been different." Possibly. But it is difficult to account for the disaffiliation of America without also examining the impersonal factors of distance, poor communication, and the tendency of cousins with similar values to quarrel, when they quarrel, with special vehemence.

Only in her discussion of America's folly in Vietnam does Tuchman make a clear case that the folly was preventable, or at least reversible. She correctly insists that it was not for want of clear warning, or minatory example (the earlier French failure to reconquer Indochina after 1945) that the United States plunged ahead in Vietnam. As early as November 1961, John Kenneth Galbraith was warning President Kennedy from Saigon that the struggle there was "a can of snakes." The warnings mounted, but they went unheeded if not unnoticed—Mrs. Tuchman sometimes seems to imply that warnings not taken were not noticed. "It is," she concludes, "a dismaying fact that throughout the long folly of Vietnam, Americans kept foretelling the outcome and acting without reference to their own foresight."

In none of the episodes studied in *The March of Folly* was it rational or wise to persist in what growing evidence said was folly. Why, then, did the makers of these flawed policies soldier on? Because, Barbara Tuchman argues, of their infinite capacity for making fools of themselves. But that is tautological—to say that men commit folly because of their proneness to act the fool. And here we get to the core of one of Mrs. Tuchman's few but serious flaws as an analyst of the past. A very great deal of history will conceal its secrets from rationalists, and she was a rationalist of the strictest sect. Nothing taxed her patience like stubborn, proud, stiff-necked, foolish persistence. As we know from her fine Thomas Jefferson Lecture, "Mankind's Better Moments," her view of human possibilities was exalted and demanding. It would doubtless have been better for humankind if it had always lived up to rational expectations. But historical experience warns that passion often overwhelms rational self-interest, and not always ignobly. Was it not a sort of splendid folly that Winston Churchill insisted that England fight on against desperate odds in the spring of 1940? Hitler apparently was willing, perhaps even eager, to guarantee the British empire in exchange for the recognition of his new imperium on the continent of Europe. Yet if this Faustian bargain could be said to have been genuinely in England's self-interest, it was not seriously considered; pride and Churchill's sense of British greatness did not permit it.

There is, perhaps, one thing to be said in conclusion of Barbara Tuchman's notable preoccupation with the horseshoe nails of the past, the small but crucial factors on which events do sometimes pivot, if more rarely than she thought. There are occasions when a single freakish incident rises to the level of historical cause. A famous instance occurred during the first Confederate "invasion" of Maryland, in the late summer of 1862, when the odds in the American Civil War seemed more even than they later became. During Robert E. Lee's first of two pushes into Maryland, one of his orders of the day outlining the plan of march and order of battle was carelessly used by a Rebel officer to wrap cigars, and dropped in a field near Frederick. There it was discovered by a Union trooper and quickly brought to the attention of the Union commander, Gen. George B. McClellan. The intelligence enabled McClellan to bring Lee to battle at Antietam (Sharpsburg), in the single bloodiest day of the war and to abort Lee's first attempt to carry the war across the Potomac into Union territory. The battle emboldened Lincoln to issue his preliminary Emancipation Proclamation, putting European powers sympathetic to the South on notice that recognizing Confederate belligerency would mean aligning themselves with the

defense of slavery. Lincoln's maneuver may have forestalled intervention. Here then was a genuine horseshoe nail of historical causation, more intriguing than any you could invent. It was so freakish,
speculates Isaac McCaslin, the hero of William Faulkner's great reflection upon race and slavery, *Go Down, Moses*, as to suggest a divine objection to the Rebel cause. God might love the South,
McCaslin muses, but not slavery. McCaslin's speculation is theolog-
ical, not historical; like an Old Testament prophet, he possesses the
rare capacity to separate his own sentiments from the divine will.

What Hugh Trevor-Roper said in his witty inaugural lecture as
Regius Professor of Modern History at Oxford in November 1957
might serve as a fitting comment on the issue of Barbara Tuchman
versus the professoriat: "Time," he said, "has shown that the real
danger of a German professoriate is the removal of humane studies
into a specialization so remote that they cease to have the lay interest which is their sole ultimate justification." For resisting that specialization so eloquently, Barbara Tuchman deserves two cheers—at
least.

The Estrangement of
Martin Luther

FOR THOSE WHO aren't historians, whether by profession or ama-
teurish inclination, the mercuriality of historical reputation can be
disconcerting. Surely, says the historical literalist, a great figure like
Martin Luther, the principal architect of the sixteenth-century Protestant Reformation, was who he was, has been so from the first,
and inquiry into his life and work is an incremental process. We
simply accumulate facts until the inventory is complete. All the portrait will need after that is an occasional retouching as a stray fact
comes to light. And you can say the same of other epochal figures—Julius Caesar, Henry VIII, Abraham Lincoln, or who you
will.

As interested readers began to learn in 1983, during the five hundredth anniversary of Martin Luther's birth, the case of the great
reformer proves the instability of historical portraiture. Like the
secreted portrait of Oscar Wilde's Dorian Gray (though without
intimations of corruption), it had been changing, while the conventional figure remains the same. Heiko Oberman's recently trans-

lated biography, *Luther: Man Between God and the Devil*, is a case in point. Oberman's work, which I discuss in greater detail below, shows that historical likenesses are shifty and elusive. The angle from which the portrait is drawn, and, of course, the medium, whether of photographic literalism or impressionism, are as important as the subject's features.

In recent decades, the catholic branches of Christendom have experienced a rebirth of interest in the early church, an attempt to recover pristine doctrine and practice. It seems a natural aspect of this revival that the latest portraits of Luther are more securely anchored in those concerns than were the heroic Protestant biographies of the past. But whatever benefits the process offers, the result may disconcert amateur readers of biography, who discover that the Martin Luther they thought they knew has become a stranger. The old Luther of liberal myth, the hero of conscience, was a more familiar and reader-friendly figure than the fiend-haunted reactionary with one foot in Dark Age superstitions that Oberman and others now portray. It may be the essence of the sense of history to savor the past in just the degree that it is strange. But accepting that takes a certain stoutness of temperament. Most of us demand biography that throws light on familiar concerns, inhabited by familiar faces.

It would not be strange, however, if the lapse of five centuries estranged us a bit, after all, from Luther. One can start with the familiar tale of his conversion: that as a law student, Luther was struck (or menaced) by lightning and abruptly decided to become a monk.

Since there have been Lutheran Yoders from the first, my own father and his ancestors, I wish I could say that the founder of the family faith is among my favorite historical figures. But honesty forbids. Luther's place in history is secure; for that matter, it should be said that Lutheranism is no more accountable for Luther's excesses (his virulent anti-Semitism, for instance) than is Anglicanism for the carnality of Henry VIII.

In the texts of my boyhood, Luther was portrayed as a heroic liberal, standing defiant before the German emperor at Worms, refusing to recant his attack on papal abuses and declaring that, God help him, he could do no other. In his *The Life and Letters of Martin Luther* (1911), Preserved Smith definitively summed up the ortho-dox liberal view: "The stake he played for was not his own life, nor even the triumph of this religion or of that: it was the cause of human progress. The system against which he protested had be-come the enemy of progress and of reason; the church had become hopelessly corrupt and had sought to bind the human mind in fet-ters, stamping out in blood all struggles for freedom and light."

Persecuted rebel, hero of individual conscience, foe of church corruption and superstition, the Wittenberg scholar embodied all that was good and enlightened in modern thought. That was the good Luther, and he came straight out of what the Cambridge his-torian Herbert Butterfield famously called "the whig interpretation of history," an interpretation that celebrates winners over losers, and progress over reaction. If such a storybook history could with-stand careful inquiry, the world would be a simpler place.

In fact, however, both the necessity and effect of Luther's revolt are now debated and debatable. We needn't worry about modern investigations that tend to cheapen the Reformation by reducing Luther or Protestantism to chance byproducts of neurosis or dys-pepsia or the effects of a tyrannical peasant father—as, for instance, in Erik Erikson's brilliant study, *Young Man Luther*. Erikson's argu-ment is that Luther's gloomy and whimsical God, so far beyond the human scale of virtue, is, in good Freudian fashion, a projection of Luther's harsh and demanding father. A student of mine once began a brilliant reminiscence by writing of her father, a Presbyte-rian parson: "I was nearly 21 years old before I began to understand the difference between God the father and God my father." Still, I detect more theology than psychology in Luther's God. And, speaking of caricatures, there is John Osborne's play *Luther*, which makes Luther an extension of his digestive tract. These modernist speculations are entertaining, but Luther finally must be taken at face value: a man of great spirituality, zeal and intellect who carried his revolt somewhat farther than he had at first intended.

The story began with the sale of "indulgences," certificates of time served in Purgatory, purchasable in coin. In 1517, when Lu-ther attacked the papal traffic in indulgences, Pope Leo and his bankers were raising funds to rebuild St. Peter's in Rome. The cause was better than the means. But Luther's indignation about indulgences led him to search for the biblical authority for penance, the sacramental activity underlying the doctrine of Purgatory. Finding none, Luther eventually concluded that many traditional claims by priest and pope, indeed all but two of the seven traditional sacraments, were nonscriptural impostures. Indulgences proved to be the string which, once pulled, tore open the fabric of church tradition.

Luther's contribution, by both scholarship and example, was flat equality in the interpretation of Christian doctrine and practice— every man his own priest. His translation of the German Bible made easier the inquiry that all were entitled to make for themselves. Scriptural authority, privately interpreted, became the touchstone. This radical subjectivism—though surely not intended by Luther—demolished Christian unity, or what remained of it, presumably for good.

Like all stories of revolution, Luther's is a story of gains and losses. When Luther assailed the authority of the pope, he incidentally pushed open (or widened) the door to the powerful secular state and thus to nationalism. He also inaugurated a new phase in the eternal battle in the church between canonical tradition and private judgment, or "conscience," as Protestants prefer to say. Had Luther and the other reformers limited their attack to clear abuses, they might have carried with them the great humanists Erasmus and More, who had been sympathizers with the first phase of reformation, and might have reformed without atomizing the church. That, at least, has been the romantic view of Catholic apologists like Gilbert Keith Chesterton and Hilaire Belloc, writers as tendentious in their apologetics as Luther at his most militant. The Chesterton/Belloc alternative probably gives far too little weight to the other centrifugal forces of Luther's time—the invention of movable type and the explosion of printing, global exploration, the stirrings of modern science. But with Luther there could be no half measures. That single-mindedness and willpower are the strength of the revolutionary. The revolutionary's weakness is that he seldom appreciates, in time, the delicate tension between authority and autonomy, custom and change, that so often yields the finest fruit of mind and spirit.

Meanwhile, something strange, even shocking, has befallen the heroic Martin Luther that most of us encountered in History 101. The new Luther isn't the only heroic figure, the earliest prophet of modernity, to undergo estrangement at the hands of historical specialists. But if Heiko Oberman's biography heralds a trend, Luther's metamorphosis may eclipse all the rest. And I don't mean a slippage in his historical importance—though that could be one result—so much as an alienation from the ordinary assumptions of twentieth-century minds.

Those of us who made our first acquaintance with Luther in the age of historiographical innocence beheld what was, in most respects, a recognizable figure—one who would be no stranger among World Council of Churches liberals and ecumenicists. His cry of defiance at the Diet of Worms in 1521 could be seen as marking a pivotal moment of release from medieval obscurantism. "Here I stand; I can do no other" sounded the high note of tolerance and variety of which our own time was the ultimate consummation. This, like the recovery of classical learning in the Renaissance, and with it the rediscovery that man could be the measure of things, was one of the standard propositions of textbook history. Now, if Oberman's portrait is to be taken as representative—and its German edition was highly praised—almost nothing of the earlier Luther survives. Instead of looking forward to the consequences of Luther's revolt, instead of taking his measure of Luther's significance from what followed, Oberman for the most part orients his examination in what lay "behind" Luther. He finds Luther's basic orientation not in some futuristic vision of the free conscience but in medieval orthodoxy.

But the reinterpretation of the great defiance at Worms is not the half of it. With the painstaking exactitude of Germanic scholarship, Oberman's most astonishing transformation is of Luther himself, the man and his character. He emerges as just that sort of medieval monk we might once have pictured as a typical target of Luther's scorn. His notion of the church is literally primitive; it is the reclusive church of the martyrs and early fathers, awaiting an early apocalyptic doom. For Luther, Oberman says, the antithesis of a "reformation" would not be a reassertion of papal authority; it would be "deformation," the clutter, sophistication and corruption that had crept into the administrative machinery of the church at the Renaissance. Oberman's Luther, though sufficiently bold to defy the dogma of priestly celibacy, married a fugitive nun and therefore looked forward to the birth of his first child with dread. He believed that God punished defiance by making monsters of infants, sending them into the world "scarce half made up," like Shakespeare's Richard III. Not only is Oberman's Luther not exactly forward-looking; he feels himself to be in hourly, daily, and always intimate duel with the Devil, a fiend who, certainly a spiritual and perhaps a corporeal presence, reveals his hand in all who differ from Luther, especially papists and Jews. The passionate and haunted sense of being "between God and the Devil" (in the words of Oberman's subtitle) explains the violent, sometimes vulgar force of Luther's rhetoric. Even Erasmus and the other humanists with whom he had at first made common cause in biblical scholarship in time drew his wrath.

In few important respects does the Luther Oberman has retrieved from whiggish history resemble the heroic liberal we once thought we knew. To be sure, his Luther still denounces unscriptural sacraments, still defies the authority of popes and councils and places scripture at the center of revelation. He still emphasizes faith and grace, not works, as the key to the divine scheme of salvation. His guidebook is still St. Paul's letter to the Romans. And, finally, Oberman's Luther remains a philosophical nominalist, scornful of the hairsplitting philosophical refinements of scholasticism. His eucharistic doctrine, "the real presence," reflects Luther's towering impatience with philosophical subtleties and "explanations" dwarfed by the majestic scriptural reality of God.

On the whole, Oberman's study presents a Luther likely to appeal to those with some patience for historical hairsplitting. But it has a rather more general significance, for it offers evidence of the specialization of the craft of history, whose effect is often to substitute complex mosaics of scholarship for color and causation, drama and heroism. Perhaps this is a gain for historical authenticity, depending on what you mean by that term—sound history must surely begin with a sense of the strangeness of eras now lost to us, whose features we are prone to view with the distortions of present-mindedness. But at a price. If you're seeking inspiration, you won't find it in Oberman's Luther. What you will find is the confirmation of a curious paradox—that the more closely history and biography approach the strangeness of the past, the less excitement they generate for the lay reader, and therefore the less intelligibility about the past they will convey. In this, perhaps, history is a bit like translation, of which it has been wittily said that "like a mistress, if it is faithful it is not beautiful; and if it is beautiful it is not faithful."

Church and State in Oxford

I CAN'T PRETEND that the historical interests surrounding John Henry (Cardinal) Newman and the other figures of the Oxford Movement of the 1830s and 1840s were uppermost in my mind when I studied in Oxford in the mid-1950s and walked the streets haunted by their spirits. A friend once took me to a service at Pusey House, a citadel of Oxford Anglo-Catholicism, which he described as "the highest church in the world." But beyond offering a certain aesthetic pleasure, the experience left little impression. Most of my friends of an ecclesiastical turn of mind were reading and discussing Geoffrey Faber's book *Oxford Apostles*, an early forerunner of the later fashion of psychobiography. Faber answered difficult spiritual questions by "explaining" spiritual interests in psychoanalytic terms. But the story of Newman and his followers is far more interesting than I supposed then.

When Newman, as a young fellow of Oriel College, Oxford, contemplated the Church of England of the 1830s, it seemed to him, as to the other polemicists he would shortly enlist to write the so-called *Tracts of the Times*, an institution in danger of spiritual death. For all its ancient strengths and beauties, it was in danger of becoming a domesticated creature of reform politics. The only alternative force within the church was evangelicalism, in which Newman's own family (like that of the historian Thomas Babington Macaulay) had been deeply involved. But to Newman it seemed an unsatisfying alternative, bent on further protestantizing Anglicanism and uprooting the church from the apostolic tradition. The foreseeable end, Newman thought, would be the church's alienation from authentic catholicity and the wellsprings of the early church. And that would entail what was, for Newman, the ultimate temptation: subjectivity of judgment. It was imperative to rekindle the now thinly stretched tie that led back to the church fathers and early Christianity.

It was not Newman but his young friend John Keble who sounded the first alarm. On the occasion of the yearly Assize Sermon in July 1832, a customary address to the assembled judges of the realm, Keble preached on "national apostasy," and the result was electric. Keble's sermon was the event from which Newman dated the beginning of what came to be called the Oxford or Tractarian Movement. The mission of the Tractarians to the church lasted for the better part of a decade, until Newman, in his sensational Tract 90, attempted to demonstrate that the Articles of Religion of the Anglican Church were more catholic in doctrine than anyone had ever supposed they were. Given the still anti-Catholic tenor of the time, these were appalling and fighting ideas, their danger shortly to be confirmed to the satisfaction of Newman's detractors by his defection to Rome.

But what, exactly, had Keble meant by "national apostasy"? What was it in the political currents of the day which the Oxford apostles resisted? By 1832, reform fever was raging in England. Parliament had just been purged by the first great Reform Bill of its "rotten boroughs," the unrepresentative seats controlled by great landed magnates. The larger towns were given the vote, and with these measures came enhanced political influence for the growing industrial middle class. The Church of England looked like the Whigs' next target. With their relaxed view of ecclesiastical policy, the Whigs envisioned a national church of broad doctrinal views that would embrace people of every Protestant inclination. There was some sentiment for the abolition or modification of troublesome historic creeds. Parliament had just abolished ten Anglican bishoprics in Ireland. They had been regarded as parochial outposts of the Anglo-Irish Ascendancy, not ministering to the Roman faith of the Irish masses. This vision of a broad church, reshaped on rationalist lines, was what above all aroused the keener high churchmen of Oxford University.

From an American perspective, the most striking aspect of this story is the Erastian tradition in England of that time, the placid acceptance of state control of the church, its creeds and structure. This control was the result of a complex history, and it had the far from negligible virtue of having produced a long period of sectarian peace. England had escaped the twin, and mutually inflammatory, defects of clericalism and anticlericalism. The parsons of the established church were expected to be learned gentlemen as well as priests, and, at the time of Newman's emergence as the prophet of a new order, even the word "priest," with its vaguely Roman overtones, was sparingly used. Many a vicar or bishop knew more of foxhunting and estate management than of ecclesiastical history. The novels of Anthony Trollope offer keen and discerning portraits of both the best and worst of the breed.

Now suddenly arose these Oxford dons, most of them young men in their early thirties, asserting the church's ancient titles as a sacred body, ordained by God, not by men. Either the church was catholic and apostolic, as the creeds proclaimed, or it was a mere civic cult, resembling the civil religion of the French Revolution, which Parliament could shape according to its own whims.

But why in 1832 and not long before? It was true that Sir Thomas More had submitted to martyrdom in the time of Henry VIII rather than take the oath of supremacy to the king. But he had been careful in his lawyerly way not to deny that supremacy. By 1832, Whig reforms had opened Parliament to "dissenters" and even to nonbelievers, who could now participate in decisions about the structure and the creeds. The Erastian arrangement had been tolerable so long as all voting members of Parliament were formally

Anglican. But now the church's destiny was subject to the arbitrament of outsiders, and, if infidels had a voice in its future, where might reform end? Was the church a loose association of pious volunteers to be buffeted by the winds of secular fashion? Or was it divinely inspired, the Body of Christ, the creation of the apostles and church fathers? These were hardly new questions, but no one had posed them so fervently or pointedly as Newman, Pusey, Keble and the other Tractarians.

To the Whig-minded, and even to quite a few Tory country gentlemen, it all seemed a dangerous and unsettling business. After so many blood-sealed compromises, the Church of England was not structured so as to satisfy a strictly logical mind. Though not its middle name, anomaly was central to the church's character. Historically "Protestant," as the term had been understood early in the reign of Elizabeth I, its liturgical forms were "Catholic," deriving from medieval forms, while the 39 Articles of Religion were, it was assumed, Calvinist. Newman for the first decade of his movement struggled mightily to braid these disparate strands of tradition into consistency—an effort that was to fail for him and for the closely watching authorities in Oxford who saw the Tractarians as foes of sound doctrine and good order.

Those who have read Newman's *Apologia Pro Vita Sua*, or other classic accounts of the movement, are familiar with the sequel. Official Oxford rose in fury against Newman and his followers after the publication of Tract 90, in 1845, argued the catholic origins of the Articles of Religion. Newman, meanwhile, was tortured by his suspicion that the Church of England was schismatic and that true catholicity lay exclusively with Rome. When Newman converted in 1845, many others influenced by his preaching and writing followed. It was a time of great bitterness and anger, nearly inconceivable in our age of ecumenical blandness and spiritual indifference.

But Newman's conversion, the most famous of the nineteenth century, initiated his true career as the century's greatest defender of the claims of religion. Newman, as Ian Ker's big new biography shows, became the mediator between the apostolic faith and the confusions arising from science, political reform and revolution. As he had earlier searched for a "via media"—a middle way—for Anglicanism, so now he brought precision and learning to controversies that were, and still are, more usually marked by inaccuracy and ignorance. Because the kingdom with which he dealt was, by the decree of its founder, "not of this world," Newman has sometimes been represented as a sort of clerical reactionary. Ker demonstrates that this is far from the truth. In due course, Newman formed a firm alliance with the so-called Liberal Catholics, rallied by Lord Acton and others against the proclamation of papal infallibility. The new pope, Pius IX, in his "Syllabus of Errors," swatted at the chimeras of political progress and science and attempted to buttress the secular power of the Vatican in the wake of the Italian unification movement. Newman and Acton thought it all misguided; for a claim of infallibility was sure to be misinterpreted in exactly those arenas in which the church's authority was strongest: matters of soul and spirit.

Newman's voluminous writings were often the offspring of tasks and controversies, but they still carry a powerful jolt of pertinence. Beautifully composed, searching and eloquent, they deal with every major predicament that religion and society faced in his day and face still—the relationship between church and learning, between intellect and spirit, between science and faith, between scholarship and biblical literalism. In subtlety and penetration there is nothing quite like them in English. Newman remains the towering prophetic figure of the nineteenth century and deserves today to be revered in both the two worlds he influenced and enriched. He was the founder of the renewal movement in Anglicanism, without which today it might well be far less than it is. And he was the prophet of another renewal within the Roman church, those reforms wrought in our own time by John XXIII and Vatican II.

One afternoon in 1983, during the 150th anniversary year of the Oxford Movement, I wandered into St. Mary's, the university church in Oxford, where the Oxford Movement began, where Keble preached his sermon "National Apostasy" that July day in 1832 and where the young Matthew Arnold (and many others) had listened, spellbound, to Newman's four o'clock Sunday sermons. Years later, Arnold recalled "the charm of that spiritual apparition, gliding in the dim afternoon light through the aisles of St. Mary's . . . and then, in the most entrancing of voices, breaking the silence with words which were a religious music—subtle, sweet, mournful." No ghosts of that time haunt St. Mary's now. There was only the late-afternoon bustle in the brass-rubbing shop, while outside, on the High Street, trucks and buses labored along with an endless growl of motors and grinding of gears. Only a heroic leap of imagination could recall the rural quiet of 1833 and Newman's sermonic music.

But Arnold was onto something. The Tractarians were priests and poets of exceptional power, and it is remarkable how few Victorian writers escaped the touch of the Oxford controversy. Not only Arnold, but George Eliot, the Rosettis, Walter Pater, Matthew Arnold, and J. A. Froude, among the historians—all felt its spell. It was a formative force in the sensibility of the Victorian age, secular as well as religious, and in later years even William Ewart Gladstone, the great Liberal prime minister, was as deeply committed to its principles as he was to political reform.

Newman's highly allusive *Apologia* requires some grasp of the controversy to be understood, and the best and clearest account of the background is to be found in one of its earliest historical landmarks: R. W. Church's *History of the Oxford Movement*. Church, who ended a distinguished career as dean of St. Paul's, had been a student in Oxford when the crisis came in the 1840s. He had deplored the blindness of the university authorities to Newman's virtues and to the merits of the Tractarian case. He viewed the dismissive treatment of Newman and his followers as a dark day in the history of the university. His book, written in old age and published, unfinished, after his death, is a historical classic, sympathetic in judgment and vivid in portraiture. But the most vital of all the eyewitness chroniclers was the skeptic James Anthony Froude, the historian of Reformation England. As a young man in Oxford he had followed Newman, with Arnold and others. ("Credo in Newmanum," he reports, was an Oxford saying of the time.) Later, as a freethinker, he renounced holy orders and scandalized biblical literalists with his autobiographical novel, *The Nemesis of Faith*. His older brother, Hurrell, had been a friend and disciple of Newman's and among the major leaders of the movement before his early death in 1836. His published *Remains*, diaries and letters posthumously edited, fanned the fear that Tractarianism was crypto-papist, an alarming supposition at a time when Roman Catholics were just casting off the age-old legal disabilities. Among other indiscretions, Hurrell Froude pronounced the Reformation "a broken limb, badly set," which would require rebreaking and resetting. His younger brother soon reached the conclusion that Hurrell and others were mistaken about the Reformation and attempted to refute their historical errors in his vast *History of England*. Meanwhile, in his *Short Studies in Great Subjects*, he told the story of what he called "The Oxford Counter-Reformation" in a mellow, amiably skeptical account, notable for its view that both the Tractarians and their foes were "extremists," blind to the inner genius of Anglicanism.

In my brief visit to St. Mary's on the eve of the sesquicentennial, I couldn't help wondering what it all came to. Was it merely a turbulence of ecclesiastical reactionaries, romantics weaving a storybook church from thin air? Although it was of great significance in the history of Anglicanism, the Oxford Movement remains an esoteric topic of the utmost obscurity for most people, often confused with the later "Oxford Movement" founded in the 1930s by Frank Buchman and known now as Moral Rearmament. Perhaps it tends to be obscure because the idea of religious development is not widely appreciated. It was Newman who demonstrated, while still in Anglican orders, that Christian doctrine is itself a historical, that is, historically conditioned, phenomenon, that it develops and evolves. Most conventional churchgoers like to think of the faith as static and rarely stop to speculate what the Church of England and its affiliated branches around the world would be like without Pusey and Newman, who restored its links to pre-Reformation traditions. Today those ties are taken for granted. That was not always the case.

The affinities between the earlier romantic movement in poetry and the Oxford Movement in spiritual matters has often been remarked upon, but romanticism is not a reliable guide to the spirit of the movement, or to the related revival of ritualism and Gothic architecture that followed. Its leaders were men of an austere spirituality and lofty if cloistered piety and idealism, determined to save the national church from smothering political control.

From a more parochial American perspective, the conflict begun in England by the Oxford Movement seems a testimony to the abiding wisdom of James Madison, the first English-speaking statesman of stature to imagine a radically new relationship between church and state that went well beyond mere "toleration." Under his First Amendment, the two would be understood to occupy parallel and separate spheres. Madison's assertion of the essential privacy of religion was a far cry from John Keble's high-church vision of the Christian society in which the church stands as the state's spiritual guardian and guide—or, at the other extreme, where it is conceived as a mere civic institution.

For complex historical reasons, the British constitution takes a very different view of the church-state relationship from our own. But the Oxford Movement began as a protest against the treacherous intimacy of the two. Had Newman and others not raised their voices, Whig reformers might well have transformed the church into a department of the state, a bureau of spiritual well-being and civic piety. The Oxford Movement was right about many things, but above all in this: dependency on the aid, manipulation and solicitude of politicians is a treacherous standard for an institution "not of this world."

Faulkner, History and the
Black Family

FOR THOSE OF US who esteem William Faulkner as the greatest of
southern storytellers, one whose pages are crowded with historical
implications, there is less mystery than many sociologists profess
to find in the recent disintegration of black family structures. For
Faulkner it was foreshadowed sixty years and more ago, especially
in what is perhaps his greatest novel, *The Sound and the Fury*, and
not there alone.

I am prompted to make this assertion by recent reports of sky-
rocketing illegitimacy rates, white and black, especially the latter.
What was considered too shocking for candid discussion only a
quarter century ago is now becoming a sort of national norm. For
black Americans, as of 1991, the illegitimacy rate surpassed 63 percent. For whites, it is almost 18 percent.

In what became known as the Moynihan Report in 1965, Sen.
Daniel Patrick Moynihan of New York, then a Harvard sociologist
serving as a subcabinet official under President Lyndon Johnson,
noted that a quarter of all black children were being born out of

wedlock. He speculated on the origins of the trend and its implications for the future stability of black families, a future which he considered alarming insofar as it was sure to leave so many young men fatherless. But Moynihan suffered the usual fate of prophetic voices who not only bring bad news, but bring it early and insist on asking why it is bad and what it might portend.

Moynihan was denounced and his concerns dismissed as incipiently racist—the more so, since he speculated that this pattern of family instability might be rooted in patterns lingering from slavery. In some times and places in the Old South, mainly when the overseas slave trade ended and the cotton boom began to open the territories of the "old southwest" to plantation agriculture, the institution of slavery placed a premium on the breakup of slave families. But Moynihan's angry critics countered that there were also stable marriages under slavery. That was also true, but mostly no one wanted to discuss the subject.

After more than three decades, what was disturbing then is a commonplace now. In Moynihan's own words, we have "defined deviancy down," in this and other ways. There is no evidence that the problem is diminishing.

No doubt the causes are many and varied. But I began by mentioning Faulkner's novels, in particular *The Sound and the Fury* (1929). For alert readers, this and other Faulkner tales are rich sources of historical insight and explanation of what has happened to black families. *The Sound and the Fury* tells the harrowing story of the decline of the proud and prosperous Compsons. The only character who preserves dignity, humanity and order in the collapsing Compson household is Dilsey, the family's faithful black servant, cook and organizer. She may be modeled on Faulkner's own Mammy Caroline Barr, to whom he dedicated the great meditation on slavery and its legacy, *Go Down, Moses*.

For present purposes, the point is that while we know a great deal about Dilsey and her virtues, and know that she has children of her own, we learn little about her family attachments, formal or common-law, as they might have been. As was not unusual in Faulkner's time in the South (or mine), she occupies modest quarters on the Compson place. Of her splendid character we learn much, but about her private life, beyond her devout religious faith, we find out very little. Dilsey is the mirror of people I knew, as the Compsons knew her. But I say "knew" guardedly. So far as those who depended on them were concerned, the faithful Dilseys of that vanished world lived in a kind of shadowland. It was the exceptional employer who knew much about the detailed kinship relations of the black world. In this setting were fashioned some of the habits and necessities now characteristic of single-parent households.

In my childhood, and well into the age when Jim Crow laws came under determined attack, the convenience of many a white household was served by patterns of employment and economic reward that placed black families under a special strain. There was a premium on strong, competent, often devoted black women. The status of their husbands or lovers, however, and of their children, especially if male, was often left to chance. Black men might be hired to do yard work or gardening, but only a few emerged, through undertaking, preaching or barbering, to middle-class prosperity or standing. Those of us who grew up under this dispensation did not often ponder its implications; they were perhaps too painful. Obliviousness thus went naturally with paternalism. Besides, we were not sociologists. I have no idea what legacies of social disorder we inherit from this tragic history. It would be easy to ignore it, but, as Lincoln said, we cannot escape history. If you know your southern novels, especially Faulkner's, however, the things that are now amiss in some black families would seem mysterious only if you take the view that social practices have no lasting consequences.

To write in this way about what remains even today a taboo subject is to risk mystifying younger readers, and perhaps all readers who weren't children in the still-segregated South of the 1930s and 1940s. Yet the world of black servants whose memorable description by Faulkner I invoke was "only yesterday" for southerners of my generation. That world was intimately familiar, within the limits I mention, though we weren't given to the analysis of why things were the way they were. Unless they are morally precocious, children are ordinarily too self-absorbed to muse on abstract questions or social arrangements. Certainly I was. In recent years, I have been interrogated by younger people about all this. How, they ask, could we have been silent beneficiaries of a social order now regarded as so manifestly unjust and perhaps destructive? The honest answer is that most southerners, though by no means all, accepted segregation and its customs as they breathed the available air, polluted or not; there was no practical alternative.

I have no idea how the so-called "pathology" of the black family structure originated, or even whether it is accurate or useful to think of it as a pathology. The Moynihan Report, reviled in its day, tended to trace the origins of black family problems, illegitimacy and fatherlessness to slavery, but other studies suggest that family structures under slavery were often strong. More recently, theories have emphasized dependencies created by the modern welfare state, by welfare state rules and the double-edged compassion that gives fresh meaning to the old phrase "cold as charity." Great fiction flows from the imaginative transformation of personal experience and observation. That was the source of Faulkner's Dilsey. She is neither a statistical construct nor the emblem of a type. She is Dilsey, a proud, specific and memorable woman. What is harder to trace is how Dilsey might have found time for a life of her own, and the truth is that she probably found very little of it in the press of her unending duties among the crazy Compsons. There were Dilseys in my early life. Their kindnesses to me are a significant part of who I am, and that has left me with a sense that I cannot ignore the distress of their descendants—without having, alas, the slightest idea of what realistically can be done to relieve it.

American Cities: The History
of a Reputation

ᕦ

IT IS ALWAYS EASY to make a case against the American city—easier, if the city is in part of the "rust belt." You simply imagine a con-glomeration of high-rise office buildings, as conventional and often as unappealing as if they'd been hatched from a universal modular mold, occupied during the day by lawyers, bankers, accountants and stockbrokers but deserted and eerie by night. You connect it by crowded auto-commuting corridors to suburban enclaves, grouped around golf courses, whose adult residents play games (when they aren't at cocktail parties) and worry about the boredom of their children. The children, meanwhile, are at the malls, or, when some-one's parents leave town, at beer busts. Divorce rates are high; so is the enrollment in churches of a theologically rudimentary sort where modern ambiguities can be forgotten or at least ignored for an hour or two on Sunday morning.

To reach these enclaves, you pass hollowed shells of public hous-ing, remnants of the livelier hopes of the 1940s and 1950s. On spring and summer evenings passing commuters with sharp ears might hear gunfire. In these fearful streets, rates of unemployment, welfare dependency, illegitimacy, drug addiction and trafficking are astronomical, and the only intruding presence is that of police squad cars, creeping through and offering nothing like the influence for social order of the old foot patrols. Occasionally, residents of all parts of the city may escape their confines along a strip of look-alike fast-food restaurants and gas stations—the Taco Bell/McDonald's/Exxon corridor—leading to a modern airport. If you flew into it blindfolded, you could not readily distinguish it or the access road from any other of hundreds.

Of course, gross caricature does less than full justice to the variety of the modern American city, especially if the city is one of the older river towns whose origins predate railways and interstate highways. If it has been fortunate enough to escape the attentions of city planners, its old buildings may even be under restoration in the process known as gentrification. Perhaps the flight to the suburbs has been offset by a pioneering reinvasion of the inner city by children of affluence whose suburban upbringing has made them search for something a bit less soul-deadening than the homogeneity and conventionality of the exurban life.

There are alternative cityscapes. Let's imagine a couple.

One is Florence—a city now more than a thousand years old with a rich civic legacy. On a mild autumn evening, the streets pulse with the corso, the nightly stroll characteristic of Mediterranean cultures. The city is dominated by the magnificent Duomo and the squares by illuminated statuary. But quite apart from these physical features, there is a sense of coherence and vitality that has vanished from most modern American cities. I saw these scenes while reporting on a meeting of American and Italian state and city officials in 1987. The Italians marveled at urban initiatives in America that needn't be cleared with a bureaucracy such as the one in Rome. The Americans marveled at an old city so enchanting, so beautiful and so full of vitality that the age of the sewer system almost seems an irrelevance.

Another cityscape I have in mind is Greensboro, North Carolina, in the 1940s when I was a boy growing up nearby. Often on Saturdays my parents would drive into the city to shop, to see movies, to visit friends and relatives. Our route passed through the eastern reaches of the city, then as now a mainly black community. Colorful masses of people, many in Saturday finery, spilled from the shops into the sidewalks and from sidewalks into the streets, celebrating the week's end. A white family felt no fear, no sense of distance, in their midst. But it was not much more than a decade later when this teeming cityscape, so congenial and colorful to the eye of a boy, was redesignated a "slum" and for the very best of civic reasons subjected to "clearance" and "urban renewal." What had been a rich and varied urban scene, not unlike Florence in spirit, was transformed into a planned scene of green spaces, new buildings and busy auto arteries. But in the process the rich life had vanished; where "renewal" had been promised, some sort of antiseptic blight had been produced. Streets were deserted and a vague apprehension seemed to hang in the air. It was before Jane Jacobs explained in her book *Death and Life of Great American Cities* the destructiveness of the "city beautiful" vision.

The historical questions seem obvious. When and why did we form the habit of understanding the American urban scene as a pathology to be cured, and to be cured, unfortunately, by medicines that so often sapped the vitality of the patient? When and why did we redesignate vibrant, colorful communities as problems or abnormalities to be corrected by social engineering? (I do not, by the way, use the term "social engineering" in a pejorative sense.) Looked at historically, the weirdness here is an angle of perception, an attitude, that tends to define the untidy variety of city life as problematical.

   Might it be a vestige of our meliorism and puritanism? Perhaps it is, since the habit of city-bashing seems to be persistent and deeply rooted. We might sing of alabaster cities, undimmed by human tears, but the utopianism of that vision is belied by the reality. The American view of cities has ranged from ambivalence to hatred. We have waged a *kulturkampf*, a culture war, against the city—not this city or that but the city as idea and archetype. It was certainly an element in the fierce reaction to New York City's financial crisis in the mid-1970s, when the Ford administration refused to reinsure the city's faltering bond ratings. This was perhaps our revenge for legendarily rude taxi drivers and waiters, neatly summed up in the telegraphese of a famous tabloid headline: FORD TO NY: DROP DEAD. That New York and other great American cities might drop dead has been the silent wish of countless rural and small-town folk for as long as there has been an America. The cities have been depicted as dens of carnality, vice, wickedness and debauchery of every sort. But is it only the hayseed voice of the crossroads sansculotte that says so? Not at all. The anticity animus has an impeccable lineage. It was no less than Thomas Jefferson, after all, who articulated our national ideals, and no one was a more eloquent detractor of cities.

They were, he wrote in his *Notes on Virginia*, "pestilential to the morals, the health and the liberties of man." This was only one of scores of Jeffersonisms on the menace of big-city life. No great American was more urbane, but none was less urban in temperament or taste. It was Jefferson the rationalist who feared that the industrial age would turn cities from organic places of civilized life, trade and learning (like his own small colonial Williamsburg) into "piles" of people, jammed together in squalor by the appetite for manufacturing and money making. Against this, Jefferson preferred a nation of farmers, close to God, selling raw materials for manufacture and keeping its pristine virtue intact.

This primal Jeffersonian theme found its echo in familiar images, myths, legends and icons: the log cabin myth of presidential origins, for instance, and the famous "frontier thesis" of the historian Frederick Jackson Turner. In his 1893 presidential address to the American Historical Association, Turner took as his text the finding of the recent census that the continent was, at last, without a frontier of settlement. He identified the westering frontier, now closed, as the defining influence in American history, a source of self-reliance, independence of mind, individualism: not exactly urban virtues. One might add the ruralist mystique of the Populist movement. After all, the gravamen of William Jennings Bryan's memorable "Cross of Gold" speech to the Democratic National Convention in 1896 was not merely a call for free silver but the warning that without the sustaining crops of the hinterlands cities would fail and grass would grow in the streets. The enmity was reciprocated. City folks sneered at the bumpkins out there beyond the Hudson River. There were also Faulkner's Snopeses—the rural ones, at least, before they moved to the county seat and did well in banking and other trades—and, of course, Erskine Caldwell's Tobacco Road. But when the monster Popeye abducts the Ole Miss cheerleader Temple Drake, in William Faulkner's novel *Sanctuary*, where does he take her? Where else but to Miss Reba Vernon's whorehouse in the wicked metropolis of Memphis?

"The decay of the American city is now one of the pressing concerns of the nation," write Lucia and Morton White in their interesting book, *The Intellectual Against the City*. It might be a sentence out of the morning paper; the book was in fact published in 1961, half a decade before the Watts riots in Los Angeles demonstrated that all was not well in the heart of the American city. But it would be hard to find any period since the Civil War when American cities were not believed to be in decline. The Progressive movement of the 1920s (and earlier) was in spirit a revolt against the real and supposed political corruption of the city machines. Built upon the recent immigrations, the political organizations of the Hagues and Curleys exemplified urban decadence, but their real offense was perhaps that they worked, after a fashion, and often worked far better than many of the reformist city governments that replaced them. They typically featured an intricate network of payoffs and jobbery, in exchange for votes. That was far from the style of Oyster Bay and Hyde Park, whence the two reforming presidents named Roosevelt came forth to battle. When Theodore Roosevelt became a police commissioner of New York City, it was thought remarkable that a gentleman would stoop to such preoccupations, even as a reformer.

In part, this picture of the American city as a locale of extremes reflects the urge to polarize, to view a thing as good or evil, welcome or threatening, radiant or noisome, moral or immoral, pretty or ugly, when usually it is a very human mixture of all these qualities. Decay is integral to natural processes, and may be essential to great cities, too. Florence was the Borgias' as well as Botticelli's, London the place of gin mills, workhouses and slums as well as of

Shakespeare, Dickens and Dr. Johnson. St. Petersburg had Rasputin and the Kirov, Memphis the dives and whorehouses as well as the jazz places that helped produce the only truly original American art form. Cities are often immoral, but the other side of their vice is creativity. They are dirty, crowded and ill managed, but variety can be compost for what cities create.

On gloomy days, it is now becoming possible to see the city as a doomed relic of the age of industrial organization and assembly lines, which, in the new age of digital information and all its attendant gizmos, is losing its reason for being. If the *New York Times* can be delivered by satellite printing thousands of miles from New York, if the Louvre may be reproduced, picture by picture, on a small compact disc, if a digital recording of the Boston Symphony is almost indistinguishable in fine stereo from a live performance, what exactly is the point of cities as traditionally conceived?

In his recent book *The Promised Land*, the journalist Nicholas Lemann describes the two-way migratory patterns of the past fifty to seventy-five years between Chicago and Clarksdale, in the Mississippi Delta. He tracks several generations of black families as they move first to the city and then back to the South, reacting to the hazard of new fortunes. There is irony in the title, for both destinations have been, in their time, promised lands. For a long time Chicago flowed with milk and honey for black migrants displaced by the mechanical cotton picker or later by the extension of the minimum wage to farm workers. It offered the lure of fair employment in high-wage industrial jobs. But then came urban decay and deindustrialization and the civil rights revolution, and the Delta began to succeed it as the new promised land. Children and grandchildren of the original northward migration are returning in numbers to an area where new standards of racial equality, and the big federal antipoverty program centered in Clarksdale, offer refuge from the disorder, danger and squalor of the big Chicago public housing projects. Once symbols of enlightened urban policy (like the "urban renewal" projects I mentioned at the outset), these are now monuments to social engineering gone sour, and a warning against glib ideas of urban reform in the future.

But back, in conclusion, to the original question: Do we accu-

rately read the condition of cities, or do we imagine their patholo-
gies by misreading the conditions of ordinary life? Americans are
instinctive reformers and moralists, given to utopian hopes; these
attitudes are in our blood. But perhaps we need to view the evolution of cities not as a linear movement up or down along a curve of
progress or decline but as a sort of unending Promethean struggle,
whose course we should contemplate with greater modesty and less
judgment. In short, there is a historical rhythm here that might tell
us things that no urban planner can.

Epilogue: An Early
Confederate History

FOR DOROTHY WARTEN CANDLEER

I RECENTLY OBSERVED the twenty-first anniversary of my move to
Alexandria, Virginia, and realized with a start that I had now lived
in the old port city on the Potomac longer than I had lived anywhere else—even the small Piedmont North Carolina town where
I grew up. After more than two decades as a Virginian, I am
tempted to ask the question that the late editor Harry Golden, who
began as a Jewish boy on New York's Lower East Side, addressed
to his fellow North Carolina editors after editing the *Carolina Israe-
lite* in Charlotte for many years. "Am I a Tar Heel?" he asked. After
so many years north of Colonel Byrd's dividing line, I might now
ask whether I qualify as an honorary Virginian at least. I am inclined to doubt it, Virginians being somewhat more clannish than
North Carolinians. But if ancestry and even sacrifice of life had
much to do with American identities these days, I might lay claim
to such a distinction in a Pickwickian and whimsical sense.

My own Virginia history, as I am tempted to call it, has approxi-
mately as much to do with my real identity as, say, the royal ances-

185

try recently attributed by Burke's Peerage, in England, to William Jefferson Clinton upon his election as president. Burke's found the great medieval figure of Simon de Montfort somewhere in the president's ancestry. My Virginia connections are but a little less remote and considerably less grand. But the connection has recently inspired research and reflection.

The most significant figure in that early Virginia history is my great-grandfather, Calvin Logue, a Georgian by birth and commander of Company B, Wright's Brigade, Anderson's Division of A. P. Hill's Corps. He might have laid persuasive claim to honorary citizenship of the commonwealth, having campaigned on Virginia soil for much of the Civil War as an officer in Robert E. Lee's Army of Northern Virginia. Indeed, he could be said to have died in its defense in August of 1864.

This ancestor, whose remains rest among the graves of other Confederate officers in Richmond's Hollywood Cemetery, was among the better-known Georgians of his day, a man of property and learning, for before the war he had been both a justice of the Georgia inferior court and his county's first representative in the Georgia assembly. He was one of six brothers who served in the war, another of whom was also killed. We of his descendants know less than we would like about this interesting man. In the early 1920s, the family house where my mother had spent her Georgia girlhood burned, and with it probably perished the documentary links to the Civil War years. I would give a great deal to have some of the letters he must have written back from Virginia to his wife and three children, in the fine copperplate script I have found on his pay vouchers. Today, we have only a few teasing mementos, the most impressive of which is the monument to him that stands in the town square of Gibson, Georgia. The inscription reads:

> Land on which the city of
> GIBSON
> Is built was given by this
> Generous and beloved citizen
> He fought in the War Between
> the States and was killed at

Deep Bottom on August 16, 1864, and
Buried in the Confederate
Cemetery at Richmond . . .

Calvin Logue, born in Warren County, Georgia, May 27, 1823,
apparently received some rudimentary instruction in law, in Ath-
ens, under the founder of what later became the University of
Georgia Law School. His mentor, Joseph Henry Lumpkin, served
as a Georgia chief justice. Logue named his only son, my grandfather, for this presumed teacher, and I take that as interesting evidence that he owed some tribute to the man.

When the news came from Fort Sumter in April 1861, it is easy
to imagine that there unfolded in Calvin Logue's Georgia village a
scene rather like the one at Tara in *Gone with the Wind*. The foolish
and impetuous young bloods—they would not have included my
great-grandfather, who had by then reached the relatively mature
age of thirty-eight—exult in the prospect of whipping the Yankees
and must be sharply reminded by a sober realist like Rhett Butler
that there isn't a cannon factory in the South. Was there a Rhett
Butler in the crowd at Gibson, Georgia, on that spring day?

By August of that year, Calvin Logue had put his affairs in order
and by November had become a new-minted lieutenant in the
Army of Northern Virginia, at Camp Lee near Richmond. Within
less than a year—it was June 1862—he had been wounded at Fall-
ing Creek and sent to the general hospital at Richmond. The
wound must have been slight, for he was soon back in the lines.
Here, however, one has an inkling of the astonishing casualty rates
of the war. When I look at the poignant photography of Matthew
Brady and others, when I read contemporary descriptions of what
the Confederate army was like, I find myself wondering how my
great-grandfather must have looked in those hard-pressed, ragged,
hungry days with Lee. If he was a true Logue, he was of middling
height, wiry, with a roundish rubicund face and, very probably, a
thatch of prematurely gray hair.

Until recently, a few forlorn facts and dates of the foregoing sort,
glossed with speculation, were about all we knew of Calvin Logue
and his military adventures. I have long had a copy of the speech

my uncle, his grandson, delivered four decades ago when the monument to him was dedicated in Gibson, on the occasion of the county centennial. The county had commissioned this memorial to him, its principal philanthropist. My uncle, an admiral and surgeon in the navy, gave a brief sketch of the strategic setting in which the seige of Richmond unfolded. He had added a few unexceptionable patriotic sentiments: "These gallant men were fighting for an ideal, for a principle, for a belief. They were fighting to protect a way of life and in their eyes they were fighting to repel unconstitutional invasion of their homeland. May the spirit, the unselfish devotion to duty, the love for one's country, his home, his loved ones, so gloriously exemplified by my grandfather . . . live with us in these days of international crisis, for without it surely there can be no hope."

Then one day not long ago I happened upon a *Washington Post* story about a Civil War historian, Bryce Suderow, who had taken a special interest in the two battles of Deep Bottom and was writing guidebooks to them. Suderow had recently arranged a meeting at the battle site between the descendants of two officers who had clashed there. One had been killed on the day of my great-grandfather's death, August 16. According to John F. Harris's account from Richmond in the *Post* of November 18, 1990, the families of Gen. John R. Chambliss, Jr., and Lt. Samuel E. Cormany had met "to let bygones be bygones" after 126 years. "Cormany, a Union officer . . . ordered the shots that killed the rebel Chambliss. . . . In a moment that spanned the ages, two great-grandchildren of Chambliss and Cormany met for the first time . . . and posed for photographs by crossing two Civil War swords in front of them." Harris noted that "like many Civil War battlefields in Virginia, those east of Richmond are threatened by the push of suburban development. . . ."

I called Suderow and told him of my own ancestral connections with the battle and the day. He turned to his computer. "Yes," he said, "there he is—Company B. Wright's Brigade. Would you like copies of his war records? They're in the National Archives." Within days, thanks to Suderow, I had the eerie sensation of holding in my hands copies of old Confederate army pay vouchers, requisition orders and other records concerning Captain Logue, of seeing his signature on receipts for his ninety dollars a month (Confederate) salary and orders for cords of firewood and equipment and dress for his troops. Thanks to Suderow's researches, and a family journey to the battle site in June 1995, I now know far more about the circumstances of the Deep Bottom campaign of August 1864, the terrain and that scorching season. The strategic prize was Richmond itself, the Confederate capital, and its vital rail connections by way of Petersburg to the west and south. The classic literature of war, from Caesar to Tolstoy and beyond, muses upon the elusive link between the microcosm of the battlefield and its strategic setting. It is a paradox as ancient as warfare that men exposed to sudden death are not always given to understand clearly the objectives for which they risk their lives. Deep Bottom is a horseshoe bend in the James River, a few miles south of Richmond. It became, for several reasons, a pressure point in the seige. Key bridges crossed the river there, and Gen. Winfield Scott Hancock was sent by Grant to attack Confederate lines across the river on the supposition (it was in fact incorrect) that Lee had thinned those lines to support Jubal Early's raid on Washington.

Like the spectacular affair of the Crater explosion, which preceded the Deep Bottom battles by two weeks, this fierce fighting was finally of no immediate significance. The lines, having withstood the assault, stiffened and held through the autumn and the rainy and sleety winter and into the spring. My great grandfather must have been with his unit in the bloody battle of the Crater on July 30. That familiar story figures centrally in Bruce Catton's *A Stillness at Appomattox,* from which the following details are drawn.

Sappers of Meade's army, boys from the Pennsylvania coal mines, had dug a five-hundred-foot tunnel beneath the Confederate line and loaded a subterranean chamber with scores of pounds of black powder. The Confederates could hear their digging, as they could hear the distant church bells of Petersburg striking the hours. The aim was to blow a gap in Lee's defenses through which the Union forces would pour in irresistible strength. But it became a disaster for the attackers, in part for the freakish reason that black troops especially trained for the vanguard were sent to the rear at the last moment, probably for political reasons. An untrained unit put in its place found itself trapped in the crater and under attack on three sides by Confederate troops. Among them, writes Catton, was my great-grandfather's brigade: "Wright's Georgia brigade . . . was supposed to charge the 50 yards of captured Confederate entrenchments south of the Crater, on the right of the Virginia brigade. The advance ran into such withering fire, however, that the Georgians were deflected to their left and came in behind the Virginians. . . ."

The misplacement of Wright's Brigade (of which Captain Logue was a part) is a reminder of the controversial reputation of its commander. At Gettysburg a year earlier, Wright had claimed an accomplishment that historians of the great three-day encounter are inclined to question—that his men had actually crested Cemetery Ridge and crossed the stone wall, the objective defended the following day against Pickett's charge. It was Wright, too, whom his corps commander, Gen. A. P. Hill, had once proposed to subject to a court of inquiry on grounds of incompetence. That suggestion drew this sensible response from General Lee: "These men are not an army; they are citizens defending their country. General Wright is not a soldier, he is a lawyer. I cannot do many things that I could do with a trained army. The soldiers know their duties better than the general officers do, and they have fought magnificently. . . . If you humiliated General Wright, the people of Georgia would not understand. Besides, whom would you put in his place? You'll have to do what I do. When a man makes a mistake, I call him to my tent, talk to him, and use the authority of my position to make him do the right thing next time."

The larger battle at Deep Bottom began two weeks after the Crater fiasco, when Hancock crossed the James and headed for the Confederate fortifications between Chaffin's and Drewry's Bluff, eight miles south of Richmond. Suderow has described the action of August 16, the decisive day for Hancock's expedition. The Confederate lines under attack by General Burney were north of Fussell's Mill, stretching from the mill pond south toward the Darbytown Road. The features of the battlefield, including the quiet pond and a farm orchard on the north side of the same country road, are easily found today and must look much as they did in 1864. At noon, four Union brigades—four thousand men—attacked the Confederate line, which gave way. As the afternoon wore on, there were several Confederate counterattacks, one of which broke back through the contested line. It was in one of these counterattacks that my great-grandfather perished. The fighting was described in the *Macon Telegraph* of August 31: "The brigade [General Wright's] was deployed as skirmishers, and the Yankees charged . . . in columns of companies, fifteen or twenty deep, and shot and bayoneted a large number in the trenches before the line, as weak as it was, gave way. Reinforcements coming up, the enemy was driven back and the works were retaken and are now occupied by our troops."

It isn't recorded, so far as I know, at what stage of the fighting that scorching day Calvin Logue died. But if heroism means anything, it must include the willingness of plain men, badly led if the information about Ambrose Wright, the lawyer-general, is correct, to fight in detail for a cause of whose reality the immediate evidence of the senses is slender and forlorn.

There is one more piece to be fit into the puzzle of my early Virginia history. On January 28, 1779, another ancestor of mine was born in Staunton. He was George Stubblefield Bruce, who went by way of Georgia to Kentucky, where others of his family had settled. Along the way he married Nancy Tompkins Weaver of Halifax County, North Carolina. Their son, Henry Weaver Bruce, born in 1809, probably in Kentucky, married Ann W. Riviere. Their daughter, Mary Margaret Bruce, married my great-grandfather Obadiah Laseter of Georgia, and the daughter of that marriage became my grandmother, Ida vandella Laseter, a great Georgia lady whom I knew well in my childhood. She was, of course, the daughter-in-law of Capt. Calvin Logue, whom she never knew since his death at Deep Bottom preceded her birth by some months. These links may seem as remote to some readers now as those interminable biblical genealogies that one hastens through in certain epochal books of the Old Testament to get to the real action. But generational connections in the South run long and deep. My mother,

born at the turn of the century, knew Mary Margaret Bruce, who
like so many of our long-lived kin survived to a ripe old age. Her
story, unlike that of the Confederate captain, seems in no respect
heroic. But she too must have borne the anguish of that time of
defeat and ruin when the South tried to rebuild from the ashes, and
without benefit of a Marshall Plan.

It is a small irony of this story that I know a good deal more about
another Confederate great-grandfather, on the North Carolina pa-
ternal side, than about Calvin Logue. Col. George M. Yoder of
Jacob's Fork, Catawba County, North Carolina, spent some of his
war years superintending—I trust humanely—a prison camp near
Salisbury. His tombstone in the old Grace Church Lutheran cemetery near Hickory gives his rank, though his distinctions, impressive
as they were, were almost completely civilian. Prof. Gary Freeze of
Catawba College, in the sesquicentennial history of Catawba
County, draws extensively on Colonel Yoder's reminiscences and
tells me that my great-grandfather was "a good social historian long
before the form was invented." In his history, in an inset entitled
"The Legacy of the Catawba Chronicler," Freeze writes:

> The most remarkable of all the early leaders . . . was [the county's] first
> historian, George M. Yoder [1826–1920]. Without him the strong tra-
> dition of public service . . . would never have developed as it did, and
> without his enthusiasm for his native place much of the county's oral
> legacy would have been lost. . . . He early became a county leader, ap-
> pointed both a magistrate and colonel of the county militia, despite his
> lack of wealth. He served briefly in the Confederate army, was part of
> the post-Appomattox county government, then was disfranchised dur-
> ing Reconstruction. After 1876, he returned to be a county commis-
> sioner and magistrate. . . . After the age of 60, Yoder became a prolific
> writer. He had listened to the stories told him by the older Jacob's Fork
> residents and began to write them—using one of the first typewriters in
> the county—for the Newton and Hickory newspapers. His pseudonym
> XYZ appeared weekly at the bottom of the neighborhood news. He also
> began chronicling the early history of the county in long essays, covering
> the Revolutionary period and the early politics of the county in a de-

tailed manner. . . . As the *Hickory Daily Record* noted upon Yoder's death, 'The old gentleman was interested in everything, it seemed, and during his long life accumulated a store of assorted knowledge that was the envy of all who knew him.' Yoder had one of the best ears for history, and its subtle nuances, in his day . . . [and] at his best could write as well as the most famous historians of the Gilded Age, including two who became president, Theodore Roosevelt and Woodrow Wilson.

One must make due allowance for Freeze's generosity, but this great-grandfather was clearly interesting. Among historians, family chronicles of the sort I have compiled here are not much in favor. But not every family has a protohistorian of George Yoder's energy or acuity. Most of us are interested in our roots, even when they fall short of the greatest distinction. Like Calvin Logue, George Yoder was a disinterested southern loyalist, though unlike Logue, so far as I know, he owned no slaves. I have in my possession a poignant photograph, taken at Grace Church one day by a Virginia neighbor whose ancestors also lie there, that clearly shows George Yoder's insistence on having his Confederate rank engraved with his name on his tombstone. His fate is to be better remembered as a local historian.

And that brings me finally back to the underlying theme of these familial researches. Their gist has little to do with racial pride, to say nothing of accord with the Confederate cause as it would have been understood in Gibson, Georgia, or Jacob's Fork, North Carolina, in 1861. For a remote descendant, the satisfaction of investigating these ancestors lies in a sense of rootedness, the establishment of a continuity with the history of a nation so largely shaped by conflict. Unlike the Rev. Gail Hightower, whose fantasy of southern triumph in Pickett's Charge is described in William Faulkner's novel *Light in August,* I have never thought that it would have been better if the tide had gone the other way on July 3, 1863, and the South had emerged as an independent nation. Still, it is an intriguing road not taken, and the surmise of my navy uncle that Calvin Logue was fighting to repel what seemed to him "an unconstitutional invasion of his homeland" has its appeal. I do not doubt that the national destiny was better served by the principle of union.

That was, after all, the view of Robert E. Lee himself until the threat to home and kin prompted him to affirm deeper local loyalties.

For those whose roots are in the upper South, moreover, there can be no retrospective cheers for secessionism, which was strenuously resisted in both Virginia and North Carolina. Yet it is strangely satisfying to reflect that some of my genes descend from the Confederate captain from Georgia, and the Confederate colonel from North Carolina, who did not passively bend to history but moved in their own ways to meet and shape it. The line that connects me to the uncelebrated Confederate warrior who rests now in Hollywood Cemetery gives me roots in what has been called our national epic, our *Iliad*. I identify myself with the old Greek who listened again and again to the catalog of names and ships from the siege of Troy. His ancestors were not, perhaps, heroic on the scale of Achilles or Odysseus. But they were among the recorded, whose lives leave small ripples and eddies in the great stream of history. When I think of this early Virginia history—and the early North Carolina history as well—I sense, however faintly, the pulse of historical consequence in my family past.

Select Bibliography

The pertinence of most of the books mentioned or quoted in this volume is explained in context. But for those who wish either to consult those works or to pursue topics they explore, the following brief and selective bibliography may be helpful. It is not comprehensive—in fact, it is entirely idiosyncratic and mirrors my heavy debt to writings in the field of history which I have admired or have been stimulated by.

Acton, John E. E. D., Baron Acton. *Selected Writings.* 3 vols. Indianapolis: Liberty Classics Press, 1985.

Berlin, Sir Isaiah. *The Hedgehog and the Fox.* New York: Simon & Schuster, 1986.

Bloch, Marc. *The Historian's Craft.* New York: Knopf, 1953.

Butterfield, Herbert. *The Whig Interpretation of History.* London: G. Bell & Sons, 1951.

Cantor, Norman F. *Inventing the Middle Ages.* New York: Morrow, 1991.

Cash, Wilbur J. *The Mind of the South.* New York: Knopf, 1941.

Catton, Bruce. *A Stillness at Appomattox.* Garden City, N.Y.: Doubleday, 1953.

Corwin, Edward S. *American Constitutional History.* New York: Harper & Row, 1964.

Current, Richard. *The Lincoln Nobody Knows.* New York: Hill and Wang, 1958.

Donald, David Herbert. *Lincoln's Herndon.* New York: Knopf, 1948; repr. 1956.

————. *Lincoln*. New York: Simon & Schuster, 1995.

Erikson, Erik. *Young Man Luther: A Study in Psychoanalysis and History*. New York: Norton, 1962.

Evans, Richard J. *In Hitler's Shadow: West German Historians and the Attempt to Escape From the Nazi Past*. New York: Pantheon, 1989.

Feis, Herbert. *Japan Subdued: The Atomic Bomb and the End of the War in the Pacific*. Princeton: Princeton University Press, 1961.

Foote, Shelby. *The Civil War: A Narrative*. 3 vols. New York: Random House, 1958–74.

Freeman, Douglas Southall. *Lee*. 1 vol. abridgment. New York: Scribner's, 1961.

Froude, James Anthony. "The Oxford Counter-Reformation." In vol. 4, *Short Studies on Great Subjects*. New York: Scribner's, 1886.

Genovese, Eugene W. *The Political Economy of Slavery*. New York: Random House, 1965.

————. *The World the Slaveholders Made*. New York: Random House, 1969.

Geyl, Pieter. *Use and Abuse of History*. New Haven: Yale University Press, 1955.

————. *Debates with Historians*. New York: Philosophical Library, 1956.

Haffner, Sebastian. *The Meaning of Hitler*. Cambridge: Harvard University Press, 1983.

————. *The Ailing Empire: Germany from Bismarck to Hitler*. New York: Fromm International, 1989.

Hexter, J. H. *Reappraisals in History*. New York: Harper & Row Torchbooks, 1961.

————. *Doing History*. London: Allen & Unwin, 1971.

————. *On Historians*. Cambridge: Harvard University Press, 1979.

Hobson, Charles. *The Great Chief Justice*. Lawrence: University Press of Kansas, 1996.

Jacobs, Jane. *Death and Life of Great American Cities*. New York: Random House, 1961.

Kennan, George F. *Russia Leaves the War*. Princeton: Princeton University Press, 1956.

——. *The Decision to Intervene*. Princeton: Princeton University Press, 1958.

——. *The Decline of Bismarck's European Order*. Princeton: Princeton University Press, 1979.

——. *The Fateful Alliance*. New York: Pantheon, 1984.

Ker, Ian. *Newman*. Oxford: Clarenden Press, 1990.

Kramer, Lloyd, and others. *How We Learn History*. Minneapolis: University of Minnesota Press, 1993.

Levy, Leonard. *The Establishment Clause and the First Amendment*. New York: Macmillan, 1986.

Malone, Dumas. *Jefferson and His Time*. 6 vols. Boston: Little Brown, 1948–81.

Namier, Sir Lewis. *Conflicts*. New York: Macmillan, 1943.

——. *Facing East*. London: Hamish Hamilton, 1947.

——. *Vanished Supremacies*. London: Hamish Hamilton, 1958.

Newman, John Henry (Cardinal). *Apologia Pro Vita Sua*. New York: Norton Critical Editions, 1968.

Newman, Robert P. *Truman and the Hiroshima Cult*. East Lansing: Michigan State University Press, 1995.

Nicolson, Harold. *The Evolution of Diplomatic Method*. London: Constable, 1954.

Oberman, Heiko. *Luther: Man Between God and the Devil*. New Haven: Yale University Press, 1989.

O'Brien, Conor Cruise. *The Great Melody: A Thematic Biography of Edmund Burke*. Chicago: University of Chicago Press, 1992.

Peterson, Merrill. *The Jefferson Image in the American Mind*. New York: Oxford University Press, 1960.

——. *Lincoln in American Memory*. New York: Oxford University Press, 1994.

Plumb, J. H. *Men and Places*. London: Cresset Press, 1963.

——. *In the Light of History*. London: Allen Lane, 1972.

Rowse, A. L. *Appeasement: A Study in Political Decline, 1933–39*. New York: Norton, 1961.

Smith, Preserved. *The Life and Letters of Martin Luther*. London: Hodder & Staughton, 1993.

Taylor, A. J. P. *The Origins of the Second World War.* London: Hamish Hamilton, 1961.

Trevor-Roper, Hugh. *Historical Essays.* London: Macmillan, 1957.

———. *Renaissance Essays.* Chicago: University of Chicago Press, 1985.

———. *Catholics, Anglicans and Puritans.* Chicago: University of Chicago Press, 1988.

Tuchman, Barbara. *The Guns of August.* New York: Macmillan, 1962.

———. *The March of Folly.* New York: Knopf, 1984.

West, Rebecca. *Black Lamb and Grey Falcon.* New York: Viking, 1940.

Woodward, C. Vann. *Origins of the New South.* Baton Rouge: Louisiana State University Press, 1951; repr. 1971.

———. *The Strange Career of Jim Crow.* New York: Oxford University Press, 1957; repr. 1966, 1974.

———. *The Burden of Southern History.* Baton Rouge: Louisiana State University Press, 1960.

Yoder, Edwin M. *The Night of the Old South Ball.* Oxford, Miss.: Yoknapatawpha Press, 1984.

———. *The Unmaking of a Whig.* Washington, D. C.: Georgetown University Press, 1990.

Index